Building Puzzles Under Water

An Autism Story

By Carrie P. Holzer

Aurora Corialis Publishing

Pittsburgh, PA

Building Puzzles Under Water: An Autism Story

COPYRIGHT © 2023 by Carrie P. Holzer

For more information, please email cori@coriwamsley.com.

Paperback ISBN: 978-1-958481-87-5

Ebook ISBN: 978-1-958481-88-2

Printed in the United States of America

Cover by Karen Captline, BetterBe Creative

Edited by Allison Hrip, Aurora Corialis Publishing

Dedicated to my mother, in loving memory of her perseverance, tenacity, and general badassery.

Special Thank You to:
Erin Drozda, Steve Wolk, and Brentwood Bank for making the dream of publishing a reality.
And to my family and friends who have loved unconditionally, encouraged tirelessly, and stood by me fearlessly.

Advance Praise

Building Puzzles Under Water introduces a bold and humorous voice to the autism conversation. Carrie Holzer's vulnerable telling of her son's story hooked me from the very start. I felt fully invested by the time Cam first climbed onto a school bus, and more so with each milestone. Readers will find in this book a source of inspiration, nuggets of encouragement, and quite a few good laughs. *Building Puzzles Under Water* is an autism story in which we all can take heart.

Amy Camp, author of *Deciding on Trails*

———

Building Puzzles Under Water may quite possibly be the most important book to a parent of a child with special needs. Carrie walks you through the difficulty of receiving Cam's diagnosis to the unexpected joys they experienced along the way. The sacrifices Justin and Gabby made do not go unnoticed either. Parenting a child with special needs requires an immense amount of love, patience, and dedication.

Building Puzzles Under Water reminds us to celebrate the milestones most of the population takes for granted. Cam teaches us the beauty in being comfortable with who we are just the way we are no matter where we are. You will laugh. You will cry. But you will NEVER put your head on your pillow at night without a smile on your face!

Genie DiChiazza, Parent of Special Needs

————

I am a single dad to a now 21-year-old profoundly autistic young man and first met Carrie through a blog I write about my life experiences with my son. I found her always thoughtful, creative, and thorough in her approaches to help Camden reach his full potential. I see all of this come alive in *Building Puzzles Under Water*.

This is such a genuine and inspirational story about life with kiddos on the spectrum, and I also find it reassuring as a parent, knowing there is always hope and opportunity. There are so many ways to feel, act, and react to this unique lifestyle as a parent, and Carrie writes about it with honesty and humor rooted in reality. This is a great read for autism parents and any parent who wants a fuller perspective on life.

Jeffrey Weinstein, Parent of Special Needs

Table of Contents

Introduction

"We can be sad about this for 24 hours, and then we hit the ground running."

I said this to my husband on the 10-minute drive home from the doctor's office where our son was diagnosed with autism. Justin was most certainly on autopilot: quiet and gripping the steering wheel tightly to get us home safely. I felt as though I was sitting just outside of myself watching another family receive and process this news: empathetic and wondering where they go from here? This family, my family. The only certainty in that moment was knowing there was just one choice to make, so we tackled it with everything we had in us. The drive home was short and yet somehow eternal. My mind was bouncing between anger, sadness, denial, and even bargaining, as if I were moving through several stages of grief at lightning speed. All the while, Cam was sitting directly behind me in his car seat kicking his feet and babbling—the past two hours already forgotten—blissfully unaware and untroubled by his diagnosis.

It was mid-March and still chilly outside. The trees were bare, and the sky was gray. It was not the exciting chill of winter beginning when the air is crisp and smells like pine; the air had been cold for too long. It had gone stale and smelled like damp wood. I was watching the shadow of trees go by through the frosted window and thinking to myself, *He's still Cam; he's the same kid he was yesterday. Don't let this change the way you see him.* I actually felt afraid to look over my shoulder at him for fear he would suddenly look different, so I kept my focus on the bare trees and my spiraling stages of grief.

As toddlers often do, Cam dropped his sippy cup onto the seat, and it rolled just out of his reach. He began to fuss. The moment of truth came, and I had to let go of the trees. I turned in my seat, caught the cup just as it was about to hit the floor, and handed it to Cam. I looked up, put my hand on his knee and saw ... Cam. My Cam. The same sandy blond hair and almond shaped eyes, a perfect shade of hazel with sparkling flecks of gold. His chubby cheeks now rosy with frustration. If he were to smile, the same little dimple on the left side of that smile would surely appear. After I handed him the cup, he once again kicked his little legs with delight as he slurped the last few drops. He didn't need to say "thank you;" the dimple appeared, and that was enough for me.

I didn't say much more on the ride home; Justin too was without words. I was anxious to get back to the house where life was simple. Two kids, two cars in the garage, two cats, one dog, and the proverbial white picket fence. I wanted to return to all the typical to-do lists to complete and errands to run. I knew things would change, but I certainly did not know just how much.

I felt heavy hearted. My inclination was to push it away, but I knew I needed to let it burn. I laid down the demand,

and I knew I only had 24 hours to feel sad. Anything more than that would be a waste of time. Once we were safely back at home hanging up coats and putting our shoes away, Cam headed straight for his favorite toys, and something the doctor said during the appointment hit me.

He will likely never speak.

I didn't have time in the office to truly take this in. Never speak? He would never tease his sister the way little brothers do or tell the mall Santa what he wants for Christmas? I simply could not wrap my head around it. How could this doctor know this after being with Cam for such a short period of time? Who the hell did she think she was anyway? Stubborn by nature, I decided that day that I did not and would not accept the "nonverbal" label. Come hell or high water, as my mum used to say, I was going to hear my kid say *mom*.

This seems like the part of the story where I should start to wonder if I did something wrong during pregnancy or during the early months of infancy, trying to find a reason or something to blame. I have to be honest: I didn't do either. I didn't see the point, and it seemed a bit self-indulgent. This was not about me, there was no changing the diagnosis and no cure, so I could not see the benefit of thinking about what I did or didn't do right. I knew very little about autism, and what I did know was because of Gabrielle, Cam's older sister. She had a friend in kindergarten with autism.

Because of their friendship, I had the opportunity to spend some time with the little boy on playdates and at birthday parties. He was very funny and loved to talk about cars. His energy was contagious. There were very obvious differences between him and his peers, but his personality was so big that was all they seemed to be—just differences.

When Cam was diagnosed, I reached out to the little boy's mom the next day. She was very intense and overwhelmed me a bit … well, actually, a lot. She invited me to her home one evening and over a bottle of wine (or two), she laid out her experiences with autism. There was so much information on everything from insurance nightmares to wraparound services that my head spun, but I too would become intense and overwhelming. Advocacy will do that to a person. In the days, weeks, and even months following Cam's diagnosis, I searched the internet for hours on end, like we do with most things these days, and found so many blogs and social media groups.

I was shocked by the number of parents and professionals out there that use the term *mourn* when talking about accepting the diagnosis. Grief, I get … but mourn? No. Let me be upfront, I am not from that school of thought. There was nothing to mourn—my child was not gone—in fact, he was right there, gathering random household items to line up in a perfect row and blowing raspberries between giggle fits. "I have not lost anything!" I would scream at the computer screen, I tirelessly looked for articles or blogs with the same attitude as my own. This sucks, I thought, so let's get to work.

Before we get into the nuts and bolts, I want to disclose that I am nervous. Many people over the years, including doctors, therapists, and teachers have told me to write about Cam's journey: to start a blog, a social media group—anything—because Cam's successes should be shared. I always said *no* coupled with some type of excuse. I've joked and said things like, "My ego is big enough already." Or I would go the busy mom route and respond, "I wish I had time, but I've got too much going on." But truth be told, I have always felt a bit scared of the responsibility of telling this story.

You will learn that Cam has overcome many obstacles; you will read about therapies and activities that worked for him; you will get a first-hand look at some of the sacrifices our family has made along the way to give Cam the best chance at telling autism to *fuck off.* (Yes, I did just say that.) My worry has always been that other parents will look at the things that have worked for Cam and think they are bulletproof. The reality is everything has been trial and error. I don't have answers, just experience. What worked for Cam may not work for the next little guy. But I have come to realize that the point of sharing this story is not the details of the trials but simply the fact that we keep trying.

You have to be open to all ideas: you keep what sticks and let go of what doesn't. But most importantly, you keep at it. Not everything you try will work but you have to try everything.

We are 11 years in, with a lot of experience and enough confidence to get Cam's story out into the world, but first, a few disclosures: I'm not a writer, unless you count the half dozen meaning-of-life poems I wrote between bong rips my freshman year of college. I swear—sometimes like a truck driver—and I am not the mom who says I wouldn't change my son for anything. I would kick Cam's autism to the curb in a heartbeat if given the chance. I would rather Cam not have to deal with it. I am also not the mom to make comments like, "Autism has made me a better person." Screw that! I'd rather be blissfully unaware of the patience it takes to be a mom of a special needs child; I'd rather head to soccer practices and chit chat with other moms about favorite wines instead of head to speech and occupational therapy and talk about autism.

That said, Cam has never seemed to mind it at all; he has always moved through it. Yes, there have been very tough times but also very rewarding ones. I will detail both the fun stuff and the hard stuff.

Inklings

Camden is our second child, and as an infant, he was pleasant. He slept better than his older sister did, hit several milestones at the same time as she did, and, in all, seemed to be a much easier baby than she was—I was thrilled (*Sorry Gabrielle, you were a delight too, I swear*). As new parents, we are focused on milestones—sleeping through the night, rolling over, sitting up, all those things that you check the books for—but it is the nuances of abnormal behavior that you do not often see in the what-to-expect books that catches you by surprise.

We are not collecting data on eye contact with our babies, their awareness when someone walks into the room, repetitive vocalizations, or wondering ... is that *normal* for a baby? Let's face it, those first few months parents are exhausted and covered in milk barf, obsessed with *when will he sleep through the night,* and *what color is his poop?* After all, that's what it should be. No one should enter new parenthood any other way other than sleep deprived and talking about shit daily.

As Cam grew through infancy, there was nothing glaring that would have tipped us off, but in hindsight, I noticed early on that he did not look at me directly when I held him or nursed him. At the time though, I thought it was a good thing. In my mind, he was interested in his surroundings: curious and observant. I did not think there was anything abnormal about it. On the contrary, I was thrilled he was so aware.

As his first birthday approached, there were inklings—little things we would see that over the next few months became concerning. I distinctly remember realizing that Cam did not seem to notice if someone new entered the room. Whether it was Dad coming home from work, Grandma or Aunt Maura coming to visit, or even Gabby waking up and joining us at the breakfast table.

Additionally, he rarely looked up from what he was doing. He didn't even seem to notice loud noises and did not react to his name being called. I had concerns with his hearing at that point, but he had passed all the hearing tests given when he was born and at his regular checkups. When it seemed others were noticing this, I played it off so no one would feel awkward. "Oh, he is playing with his toy. That's his favorite." or "He has a snack in his hand, and no one can compete with a sweet potato puff." I wanted to believe those excuses, but in the back of my mind, I was starting to take note.

By age one, Cam did not have a wide range of consonant sounds, or any baby talk the books said he should have. He had a few letter sounds that he would repeat, and I do mean *repeat*. To this day, we still hear some of those original vocalizations from Cam, but we will come back to that later. It was at this point that I started to worry that something was off. But the truth is, even within a marriage there is hesitation to be the first one to say, *There might be something going on with him.* What if you're wrong? What if your spouse thinks you are being too critical or paranoid? And the worst one ... What if you are right? It is as if you don't want to be the one to start the conversation.

I had thought about bringing up my concerns to Justin, but at the same time, I was explaining everything away in my mind. I hadn't even considered that he might be having the same concerns. Then, one day, Justin and I were sitting on the couch and Cam was on the floor lining up his cars one after another in a perfectly straight line. When he ran out, he started removing one from the end and placing it at the front of the line.

I said to Justin, "Look at how perfect that line is."

Then Justin, without looking away from our son replied, "I don't think that's a good thing, I think he might have autism."

It was almost as if he was waiting for the right moment. But at the same time, it seemed to come out of his mouth involuntarily, like a hiccup. I felt both relieved and angry at the same time; there it was, conversation started.

Justin went on to explain that he had recently watched a television show where two characters and their toddler aged sons were spending the day together. The dads were in a competition, *look what my son can do* kind of thing. Over time, it became clear that one of the little boys was achieving things that kids his age should not be able to do.

He was building over-the-top towers of blocks. As soon as he said that I thought about Cam's building abilities.

Cam was able to build towers well above his head—as far as his little arm could stretch—perfectly aligned and often intricate designs. This started early, and it wasn't just blocks, anything stackable was fair game for Cam. If he was in the kitchen, he would stack soup cans; in the living room, toys; and the upstairs hallway, toilet paper rolls. In that instant, all his builds and towers came to mind. Not once did I ever find it strange. As a matter of fact, I was beyond impressed. But as I started to examine it, I realized that it did not seem like a hobby or an interest for Cam; rather, he was so fixated on stacking, it was as though he had no choice but to build.

From there, I started to think about everyday activities that slowly became part of Cam's life, and looking back on them now, they were all signs. Camden had incredible motor skills for his age: everything from being able to manipulate small toys to running at full speed and then being able to stop on a dime. He also had unexplainable balance, which became one of the most fascinating things to watch. By the time he was 18 months old, it was not uncommon to walk into the living room to find him perched on the end of the arm of the couch, with one foot tucked under him like a flamingo and the other foot planted on the couch. He would step up onto soccer balls or basketballs in front of the tv to watch cartoons without so much as a wobble and larger toy trucks were an easy step stool to see what treats might be on the kitchen counter.

I would pick him up from his various perches with the typical mom warning, "You're going to get hurt!" and he would wrap his legs around me putting his arms out like an airplane. He would even lean back sometimes, completely balanced, and not a worry in sight. Something else hit me: he never seemed to get dizzy. He could spin in circles for minutes at a time. I would hover waiting for him to stop and topple over or veer off to one side but that never happened. He would stop and then walk a straight line to his next interest. He loved to spin.

At times it just seemed his natural state, "Where is Cam?" someone would call out.

"He is in the kitchen spinning" was typically the answer.

In addition to his love of building high towers, he also loved to line things up: everything from blocks to snacks. When Cam would create a long line of items, he would circle his creation over and over, adjusting things if necessary to be in perfect alignment. When he was satisfied, he would get down on the floor, put his cheek to the ground, and close one eye, seemingly gauging if his line was straight. It was one of those things *Cam just does,* but all of a sudden, it became something to think about. What exactly was he doing? I would eventually learn that this is a visual self-stimulatory behavior.

Cam would also look at things or people from the corner of his eyes. We called it the *side-eye* in the beginning, because to us, it was Cam being silly. "Oooh, you are getting the side-eye from Cam!" When in reality, this is another visual self-stimulatory behavior. If you try this yourself, you will find it quite uncomfortable: With your head facing forward, point your eyes to the farthest corner of the ceiling to your left or right without raising your head and try to stare at the corner where the ceiling meets the walls.

Likely this is doing nothing for you other than eye strain or even dizziness, but for Cam, this was providing something essential. Visual self-stimulatory behaviors can serve many purposes for people with autism: it can help decrease sensory overload, aid in adapting to unfamiliar surroundings, and can have a calming effect, to name a few.

Cam would do this multiple times a day for several minutes at a time. Sometimes he would look in our direction this way, or at a line of toys, but most often he would simply look at an upper corner of a room. At the time I had no idea what he was doing and to be very honest there were times that I thought it was creepy as hell.

Once, while cleaning up around the house, I walked into the kitchen to find Cam sitting on the floor in one corner of the room, his chubby little legs crossed with his hands on his knees. His eyes were pointed upwards and far to the right, staring at the corner of the ceiling, and sitting impossibly still. Keep in mind this was before his diagnosis—before I had any clue what this behavior meant. His eyes were positioned so far to the upper corner of his eye sockets that there were more whites of his eyes visible than iris. I was ready for the head spin and pea soup projectile barf.

I froze in place; my stomach rose to my throat as I stood there staring at my son. I called his name from the doorway to break the behavior, but he did not budge. It was so disturbing that I actually backed out of the kitchen slowly and called Justin, which is hilarious in hindsight. As I was telling him what was going on, my sweet little Cam got up and toddled out of the kitchen, swiping his fingers along my leg as he headed toward his block bin unceremoniously, apparently not taken over by some malevolent entity. I think Justin thought I had lost my mind. The day continued without incident, back to the regularly scheduled program of taking care of a toddler and a six-year-old.

There were other behaviors that, at the time, seemed a bit out of the ordinary, but when you're in the middle of making sure your older kid is doing her homework and keeping the dishes in the sink at a minimum (not to mention a thousand other things), those little quirky behaviors float to the back of your mind. After all, he was healthy, happy, and hitting all major milestones other than speech.

When I spoke to family and friends about his lack of speech, I was told over and over that second children often talk later or that boys, in general, talk later than girls. I remember my aunt telling me that, out of her five kids, her boys talked late, and the youngest ones even later as the older kids tended to talk for the younger ones. I can say without a doubt that our daughter was doing just that,

"Cam needs his sippy cup," and "Cam can't reach his truck," and so on. So, I was easily sold on those explanations for the time being.

Cam was also very particular about how things needed to be at a very young age: pillowcase on just right, toys in very specific spots, and highchair positioned perfectly in the corner of the dining room. His reaction was dependent upon his mood. Sometimes he would simply push the highchair back to the corner, adjusting it on his way to the kitchen to look for a snack, or you might see him shaking out his pillow mindlessly while watching cartoons.

Other times, he could get quite mad and share his frustration with a growl, a double fist pump to his sides, or—much to our surprise—a full meltdown at times. He never came to us for help. He couldn't ask for it, nor did he bring us the pillow or point out the problem in any other way. His meltdowns were never directed at us; he did not drop himself at our feet in distress. It was all very solitary.

Of course, we would step in, but that too would frustrate him at times. There was a long period of time that Cam insisted on grabbing the tea towel from the oven door handle and lay it out flat to try to fold it into a perfect square. The trouble there is once you wash those suckers, they get misshapen and never fold perfectly again. It became such an issue that I stopped hanging them on the oven all together. And it didn't stop there: sheets and blankets were another go-to for Cam. Luckily those would fold up into a nice and neat square. He would start by making sure it was spread out and smoothed across the floor. Because of the size of the sheets and blankets, Cam would sometimes accidentally flip a corner over with his foot when getting up off of the floor to walk around to the next corner and smooth it out. He would end up in this endless loop of fixing corners and smoothing out wrinkles.

It was hard to watch, sad even. We would try to help but he would get mad at us most of the time. He wanted to do it by himself, but there were times he would give in and let us help. I can't tell you how many times we folded blankets, sheets, and tea towels with him—hundreds, I'm sure. And Gabrielle too, she has never missed a beat with Cam.

I think it's important to talk about these behaviors because they are outside of what many people think are indications of autism. I came across hand flapping and tiptoe walking over and over again during those early weeks of searching the internet late into the night. Cam has never done either, yet these were the signs listed in just about every article. It gave me hope every time I read it, "Cam doesn't do that!" I would cheer while waving my middle fingers at my computer.

By the time he was diagnosed, I wanted to say, *but he doesn't walk on his tip toes!* Children with autism are still individuals, and although hand flapping and tiptoe walking are very common, there are many other behaviors that can easily be mistaken as quirks. No one can list all the possible indicators.

My best advice to anyone who has ever reached out to me with concerns about their own child is this: do as much research as possible, see as many doctors and therapists as you can, and take full advantage of any government assistance available, including early intervention programs and medical insurance coverage. Most importantly, always see your child first, possible diagnosis second. Once you have a diagnosis in hand, never be afraid to question the doctors and mental health professionals based on what you know about your own child. If you disagree with anything from treatment plans to prognosis, do not do so quietly.

First Steps

With the conversation started, I had no choice but to come to terms with the fact that there might be something going on with Cam. Eventually, I did what a lot of people do, I started discussing this with loved ones outside of our home: my aunt, my sister, my mother-in-law, and my closest friends. One after another their immediate reactions were to calm my nerves, and I think in doing so, they were calming their own.

I was met with a lot of, "You worry too much. He is fine," and, "He will catch up," responses. We inherently want the people we love to feel calm and comforted. Truth be told, by the time I started discussing this with everyone, I was convinced, and I wanted them to say *This is fucking terrible. What's next?* In a way, when people try to explain away what you are telling them, you start to feel defensive; it feels dismissive.

Talking to others brought about the same fears I had over starting the conversation with Justin. I started to think, Are you listening to me? This shit is happening. I am not making it up. I am not overreacting. The kid has been trying to fold a tea towel for 45 minutes! Don't get me wrong, I understand their reactions, and before Cam's diagnosis, my reactions were the same to others in worrisome situations. No one wants to accept that something may be wrong, and it's especially hard when you are looking at this sweet little boy toddling around the house happy as a lark. I decided pretty quickly I would keep everyone on a need-to-know basis until I had some answers. I needed to keep these thoughts close and just between Justin and me to keep myself from feeling like I was not being heard.

Just a few months prior to Cam's diagnosis, we were at the pediatrician's office. Before going, Justin and I agreed to bring up the behaviors we had been seeing. After giving the doctor the low down, he looked at Cam's growth chart, asked us some general questions about different developmental milestones, and then said, "He will catch up." This is even harder to hear from a doctor. Sure, I could have taken that answer and ran with it. Here is a medical professional telling me that he will catch up, but I was not going to leave there without being heard. I knew there was something holding Cam in endless loops of folding towels and lining up blocks. I pressed harder, and eventually the doctor said that, if we wanted to have Cam evaluated, we could utilize our county's early intervention program and gave us the contact information.

I called as soon as we got home and made the appointment. It was extremely easy. I was worried I didn't have enough information to warrant the evaluation, plus Cam was so young—only 19 months old—but to my surprise the woman on the phone did not ask many questions and was very supportive of my call.

I remember her saying, "It doesn't hurt to have the evaluation," and thinking her statement was that of agreement but also had a glimmer of hope in it. In my mind, *it doesn't hurt to …* is typically a statement pointing out precaution, not caution. The downside to the phone call was that we would have to wait a few weeks for the in-home evaluation, and I was a bit deflated because I wanted to get moving. Those days leading up to the evaluation were tough: watching every move he made, trying to stay calm with every side-eye Cam threw in my direction, and reminding myself, *This is your baby. He is not a stranger to you. Stop staring at the kid!*

Evaluation day finally came, and that morning was the same unassuming morning as always: kids up, fed, teeth brushed, dressed, and Cam and I dropped Gabby off at school, then headed back home. I was too busy with the typical morning routine to really think about what was coming next. I knew from the initial call that someone would come to the house to observe Cam, there would be motor skills testing, language, self-help, and cognitive ability testing. I felt unprepared, but there was really nothing to prepare. Clean the house and hope Cam displayed some of the behaviors we were seeing during the appointment. It's ironic how that works, especially once you are in the thick of therapies and wraparound services. You hope that your child displays enough autistic behaviors—or "autistic-y things," as we call them—during evaluations to show the *need* required by health insurance companies, and yet all the while, you are hoping to see progress. That is one of the biggest conundrums of autism for me.

As a toddler, Camden could be very solitary—not in a negative way but in an *I'm busy with my own world* kind of way. He was either open to reciprocity or he wasn't. That morning, he wasn't. I thought we weren't going to get anywhere. As I was doing a final check on the state of the house, I heard a knock at the door. My heart raced as I opened the door and welcomed the therapist into my home.

She walked in with a pleasant smile, shook my hand, and while doing so placed her other hand on the outside of mine. Something about that gesture calmed my nerves, and I was able to relax a bit. She sat right down on the floor next to Cam. I wasn't sure where I should position myself but decided on the couch so I would not be a distraction. She began talking to Cam and picking up some toys that were around him. He did not seem to be aware that she was there at first but then he slowly started to take the toys back and line them up. I thought, *OK, here we go.*

She had a large black case with her, and when she opened it, I could see block sets, beads and strings, zippers and snaps, and a handful of other colorful toys and objects. She started with fine motor skill activities, and Cam was very interested in the beads and strings and various small trinkets. She realized quickly that he could manipulate the small items with ease, and she seemed quite impressed. Next, she had him try the zippers and buttons and even had him slide on a pair of oversized socks. He nailed all of it. As the testing went on, Cam was tolerating it very well. I had fears that this was going to be tough on him, but he was a model subject.

At one point, the therapist asked me about his balance: his ability to climb, hop and spin. I laid out his balancing acts and building abilities in detail. She explained that sometimes when children have exceptional fine and gross motor skills like she was seeing with Cam, that their speech can be a bit delayed because they are using that brain power elsewhere. My heart soured and I thought, *wonderful! Case closed. Have a great day. Bye!*

But the evaluation continued. I watched her make slash marks in boxes and add short notes on the page here and there. I was trying to act cool from the couch while straining my eyes to try to read what she was writing—my own version of the side-eye. Eventually the evaluation turned to me.

A large percentage of an autism diagnosis relies on the parent questionnaire, and even though I had seen versions of it online, it was still daunting. Once I answered all the questions, she took some time to calculate and then score them. She explained the scale and then said that Cam's score was in the moderate to severe range. Between that, and her work with Cam over three hours or so, she looked at me and said that he could be on the spectrum, but she herself could not diagnose him. She gave me a list of child psychologists in the area.

Wow! Obviously, I had hoped that I was just doing my due diligence. I hoped I would be told that he was fine and that he would reach the delayed milestones in short order, but that was not the case. She explained that, if and when he was diagnosed, he would qualify for early intervention, and that he would likely receive speech and occupational therapy free of charge through the county program. I could tell she was being very careful with her words because she could not legally diagnose Cam, but she knew, and in turn, so did I.

She handed me her card and said she was very impressed with Cam. She did seem to genuinely enjoy him. Even as a little kid, when he was engaged, he was charming and affectionate. He didn't necessarily come at you with a hug, but he would at times sit next to you and pat your leg or snuggle in your lap and twist your hair around his pointer finger while he watched cartoons. I didn't quite understand what she meant when she said she was impressed with Cam, but looking back and knowing how hard Cam has always worked on his goals, I believe she was impressed by how much of the evaluation he was able to complete.

I kept a brave face as she gathered her things and said goodbye to Cam. I held my breath, hoping he would respond, look in her direction, or wave—anything that might tip his score to just moderate—one last desperate hope before she left, but nothing.

Cam typically did not acknowledge when people would enter or exit a room, and that day was no exception.

Moderate to severe.

I shook her hand and thanked her for her time. She again placed her other hand over mine, only this time it did not make me calm, and I felt my eyes starting to well up. I remember thinking, *no, don't do it*, and with that, I marched to the kitchen and hung her business card on the refrigerator before starting lunch.

Building Puzzles Under Water

Officially Official

Justin and I had chosen a psychologist from the list who was close by. I know it's strange to use this as criteria, but the truth is Cam hates long car rides, and we did not want his anxiety from being in the car too long to interfere with the appointment. Who bases this important decision on proximity? But we didn't know where to start, and removing any additional stress on Cam seemed like the way to go.

I called and spoke with the receptionist. I explained that my son had an evaluation with early intervention and that we would like to set up an appointment. She asked outright what our concern was, and I said, "He may have autism." I was surprised at how matter of fact that sentence came out after months of explaining everything away. The woman on the other end of the phone could not have known how hard it was to get to that moment unless she had experience with it herself.

On March 14, 2011, Camden was a few months shy of two years old. I had the stocked diaper bag strapped over my shoulder complete with toys, his sippy cup, and snacks to keep him placated—how typical mom of me. The three of us entered the waiting room of the doctor's office. It was tiny, the walls were beige—very beige—and faded floral paintings hung above the vinyl covered chairs and forest green industrial carpet.

I hate forest green.

We rang the bell and waited. Cam immediately wanted to bail. He was fussy and headed toward the door. I was on the same page, but we had to do this. Justin scooped him up, and I checked us in.

The door next to the check-in window opened, and a tall, rather round woman, perhaps in her mid-to-late fifties, walked through the doorway. I remember her so vividly; she had a brown tweed suit on with a cream blouse tied at the neck that washed out her skin. Her hair was perfectly styled: tight curls brushed out revealing a mix of blond and gray strands. She, without a doubt, had a "mean principal" vibe about her. I half expected to see a ruler on her desk. She seemed to size us up before calling Camden's name. We got up and followed her down a hall that was also very beige.

She introduced herself without leaving time for us to introduce ourselves and, pointing to the doorway we were heading into, said, "You can have a seat in my office."

I was put off immediately, so before taking a seat, I said, "My name is Carrie, Camden's mother, and this is Camden's father Justin."

She half smiled and continued through the door while pointing at two chairs across from her desk. No handshake, no *nice to meet you,* just a "have a seat" gesture. I could tell by Justin's posture and his grip on Cam that I was not alone in my first impression of this woman: unbelievably cold and uninviting. I thought we were in the wrong building. She could not possibly be a child psychologist, but there she was, rigid and stern and peering at us from over the top of her wire-rimmed glasses.

Cam was wriggling around on the verge of an all-out protest, and I handed him his sippy cup full of hope that would settle him. The doctor asked us what brought us to her office. We explained how we came to make the appointment: the behaviors we had been witnessing, the pediatrician appointment, and the early intervention assessment. She was shaking her head, but it did not seem she was listening to us; she had her eye on Cam who was still fussing a bit. She then started to ask us some general questions, including the milestone questions, of course. When it came to speech and communication, we had nothing to report.

Cam didn't point to things he wanted, and he certainly didn't use any words. He did not raise his hands to us to be picked up or pay attention when we entered a room. She explained that she would give us a questionnaire to complete, and as she handed it to us, she went on to say that the questionnaire was the main tool for diagnosis, so we needed to be very honest with our answers. She then asked us to place Cam on the floor. Justin set him down and I started to fish toys out of the diaper bag with one hand while holding a tri-fold questionnaire that apparently held my son's fate in the other.

She asked that we not give him the toys and to remove the sippy cup. Really? Has this woman ever actually met a toddler? To this day, I can hear her tone; it was almost as though the whole thing was a bother to her. She tried to get his attention from behind her desk by calling his name. He was just standing in front of Justin and I, trying to figure out why the hell we were not giving him his toys. She tried again, saying his name louder and louder while tapping a fingernail on her desk. I felt like saying, *He's not a dog.*

Justin and I started the questionnaire. She seemed to stop trying to communicate with Cam, so I handed him a toy—half for his sake half for mine—in an effort to regain some control of the situation. Not once did the doctor come out from behind her desk to get close to Cam or even attempt to get on his eye level.

She then excused herself and said she would give us some time to complete the questionnaire.

As soon as she left, Justin and I just looked at each other. We were both shocked, *What in the hell is this?* Justin was so frustrated. "How is this even scientific? Parents could easily answer questions with bias," Justin's whisper yelled. I was in complete agreement, but all we could do was dive in. He and I took turns reading the questions out loud while the other wrangled Cam.

It was a scaled questionnaire, and as we were going through the first part, we seemed to be choosing a lot of *never* or *rarely*. Many of the questions seemed too ambiguous like, *Does your child climb furniture without fear?* Do any kids climb furniture *with* fear? Justin's frustration was growing with these types of questions, as was mine, but we did our best to answer honestly even though some questions seemed so broad we were unsure how to answer. After some time, the doctor was back in the room with us, which made it hard for Justin and me to complain about the questions outwardly. But we eventually finished it. She left the room again with our completed questionnaire, still very little interaction with us or Cam, but by then I was happy not to have to speak to her.

We sat in silence, Mom and Dad on autopilot taking care of Cam and keeping him busy. When she came back, she put the questionnaire on her desk, placed her chubby red hands on top of it, and said, "Camden is autistic." She said it so matter of fact, as if she was telling us what time it was. That's it? A few questions and what I considered the bare minimum of observation—is there nothing more concrete? She went on to say that for early intervention services, we could contact The Alliance for Infants and Toddlers, Inc. with his diagnosis and set up therapy.

Again, as if she was simply giving us directions to the nearest gas station she said, "You should understand that Cam will likely never speak or attend a typical school."

She went on to say that Cam will need a way to communicate his needs so we should buy a tablet and install picture applications on it, reassuring us there is a large variety out there for kids like Cam.

Back then, I had never actually held a tablet or knew what she meant by "applications." I was numb. I believe Justin was too. She then instructed us to make a follow up appointment with the receptionist for several weeks out. Clearly, her way of making it known that the appointment was coming to an end.

"Do you have any questions?" she asked.

With an endless number of questions in my head I responded, "Not right now, thank you."

I could not bring myself to stay in that office with that woman another moment. With that, we headed for her door. I was so angry, and I thought to myself, *Make her shake your hand and tell her it was HER pleasure to meet you.* But I didn't. If I went down that path I wouldn't have stopped, and besides, what good would that do for any of us? I scooped Cam up and started down the hall. As we approached the receptionist window, I picked up the pace, and Justin was right there with me. Neither one of us had any intention of setting foot in that office again.

Go Time

You always hear that early intervention is the key. I could not help but wonder if we were early enough. Was it possible that we waited too long to have the conversation, and was I ready to wonder for a lifetime if our timing was off? What I *did* know was that I was ready to get moving. The very same day that Cam was diagnosed, I reached out to the woman who completed the home evaluation through the county. Her business card dutifully hung on the refrigerator next to photos, travel magnets, and grocery lists, sticking out like a sore thumb. With diagnosis in hand, we were ready to begin therapy but had no idea what that would look like.

The therapist was very patient with me and explained the next steps, paperwork for insurance, paperwork for the county, and paperwork for medical assistance. I was a bit taken aback by that. Medical assistance? She explained that, in our state, children with autism automatically qualify for assistance and that we would not have any out-of-pocket expenses for Camden's therapy. This was a pleasant surprise to say the least. I had a fleeting thought or two over those weeks about the cost of therapies but figured we would cross that bridge when we came to it.

She was so kind and thorough, and thankfully, very honest about the mounds of paperwork coming my way because, once it started coming, it never stopped. After finishing with the business side of things, she took the time to ask how we were. She was empathetic but positive in her tone and assured me Cam would have a wonderful team.

Within a few days, numerous envelopes were delivered to our mailbox containing countless forms to complete and return to the powers that be. As soon as one was delivered, I would make quick work of it and have it done and back in the mail the same day. I was not messing around, and again, I wanted to get moving. Time was ticking.

It took several weeks for everything to be processed, and eventually, I received a call from the early intervention team lead who would be handling Cam's therapy. He explained that, based on Cam's diagnosis, as well as the assessment that had been completed at home, Cam was approved for weekly in-home speech and occupational therapy. This was essentially four, one-hour in-home appointments per week. He then offered a tentative schedule. I asked if I could go ahead and approve the schedule right then and there. If I could speed up the process by agreeing to the dates and times he had just laid out, I wanted to go ahead and do that. Thankfully, the answer was *yes*. And just like that, after weeks of paperwork and waiting, we had a plan.

By this time, I had a folder of all-things autism. I wrote down the names of the therapists, when they would be visiting along with their specialties, and contact information. From there, I added all the appointments to our calendar. Cam was about to be a very busy 21-month-old. Early intervention was available to children up to the age of three. What would the next year look like?

I suddenly became aware of every speck of dust in my house, every toy on the floor, and every stain on the carpet. It was as though my brain switched gears to focus on cleaning; after all, it is easier than autism. I scrubbed, dusted, and vacuumed every surface and even touched up paint on the walls. All things I could control and see immediate results with—my kind of challenge.

But when the dust cleared, I couldn't help but wonder what life would be like. Will Cam have time to just be a kid with all these visits? And Gabby—what will she make of all of this? Will she be jealous of all the attention Cam would be getting? Would his therapy schedule interrupt her schedule of various activities from karate classes to soccer practice? Oh, wait a minute, will Cam ever have extracurricular activities like karate and soccer? Will he even have curricular activities? According to the psychologist that diagnosed him, he would not have any semblance of these typical childhood things.

My mind was all over the place during those days leading up to the start of therapy. There were moments I felt relieved that help was on the way. We were on the right track. Other days, I was angry that my son had far more mountains to climb than the average two-year-old and that his mornings would be filled with strangers telling him what to do.

At times, I was worried that the therapists would think I was a bad mom, not capable of raising my child without help. Would they secretly judge me because I thought my two-year-old loved to fold towels, oblivious to what that might mean. I kept wondering how, even with their education and knowledge, they would communicate with Cam. Would they get him? Would they be able to read his moods the way we do? Understand his unique yet very limited means of communicating? These are all things that our family gradually and naturally came to know—a truly unspoken understanding of what made Cam tick.

It was only in the weeks leading up to this moment that I realized just how many intricacies Cam's behavior held. It felt like I was handing over my son, that I was surrendering as a parent. It was as though asking for help hurt my ego. I felt like I was taking a step backward as a parent, a failure on my part. I had to check myself and understand this was not about me. It was about Cam and getting him the help he needed, which, in reality, was brave. Putting your ego aside to ask for help is not a failure; it's success.

I navigated these emotions privately. I did not want to share the side of me that was scared. The outside world would only see the mom powering through, making the appointments, and completing paperwork. No one would ever see the mom who secretly broke her rule of being sad for just 24 hours by all the days she cried in the shower or in the early morning hours while everyone was still asleep.

Revolving Door

Before we get started with all things in-home therapy, I want to let you know that I have remained in contact with just about everyone who came into Cam's world during those early years. They became known as *Cam's helpers* to us. I think it was Gabby who created the title. I talked with each of them while writing this book and asked for permission to use their first names. To my delight, nearly all of them said *yes*. I was hopeful this would be their answer as they are so important to this story, and I could not imagine using an alias for any of them. Their responses were filled with kind words and excitement, which gave me further validation that, yes, this story is unique; it is inspiring, and it does need to be told. They all became family, a support system like no other in our lives. To this day, many years after they worked with Cam, I still received check-ins and birthday wishes for him. As much as they made an impression on Cam's life, it seems his impression on theirs was equally magical. I will forever be grateful for them, and I can't wait to tell you about them.

Our first visit would be with Cam's speech therapist. The house was sparkling, with everything in its place, and I was pacing the living room and looking out the window with every lap. Cam was on the floor playing with his blocks, not a care in the world. I heard a car door shut, and my stomach dropped. A minute later came a formidable knock on the door—exactly on time. I opened the door to a beautiful young woman with medium blond hair that was tousled from the wind and big, warm brown eyes. Something about her face and her wind-blown hair was immediately familiar somehow. She introduced herself and shook my hand. Her name is Teri. Her handshake was firm, matching her knock, and I knew in that moment she meant business—not in an intimidating way—more in an I-am-here-for-you way. I welcomed her inside, as she pushed her hair away from her face, tucked it behind her ears, and placed her bag on the floor. I asked her if it was ok that I stay in the room. She was very open to it, and I promised to try to stay out of the way. She sat on the floor near Cam and introduced herself:

"Hi Cam, I'm Miss Teri."

"Are you playing with blocks, Cam?"

"Do you like playing with blocks, Cam?"

"May I hand you a block Cam?"

She picked up a block, and as she did, Cam looked up from his stack! More or less in her direction but not into her eyes. It was an acknowledgement, and Teri understood it. She handed him the block at once, and he added it to his build.

"I like where you placed the block, Cam," Teri said.

I wanted to cry right then and there. I had been so concerned about how this day would go, and there he was, open to this new person in his space. There she was, this person I had never met, giving me all the hope I needed for that day. At that moment, I decided I would find the hope in each day and run with it.

Teri did not expect Cam to answer her questions or try to force any form of communication from him, but Cam was interested in Teri. I remember watching him side-eye her as she started to remove items from her bag.

She just laughed and said, "Are you watching me Cam?"

It was obvious this was not a new behavior to her. I was giddy.

"What does Miss Terri have in her bag, Cam?" she said.

I was half expecting a magic wand. That is how impressed I was with her in that short amount of time. She pulled out a small peg board with brightly colored pegs that would fit into one another. As she was setting up the board near Cam, she started to move his blocks off to the side. To my surprise, Cam did not protest. Typically, if you moved his blocks, especially after he made his line or tower, you were in for it.

Teri began to put a few pegs on the board and placed a couple in front of Cam. I noticed that Teri kept the peg bin beside her, just out of Cam's reach. Cam began to mimic Teri by putting a few pegs on the board. Once he had used the pegs in front of him, he tried to help himself to some more leaning toward the bin with his arm stretched out. Teri picked up the bin and said, "more please," then handed him one peg. Every time Cam would reach for it, she would say "more please," then hand him another.

She started labeling the pegs in tandem, "more please," "green peg." I could tell she was not expecting him to repeat any of those words at that time because she would make the statement and hand him the peg right away; there was no pause left for him to repeat. She was simply associating the words with the action of getting another peg to add to the board. Cam caught on so quickly that instead of reaching out his hand, he started to raise his head up, as if to look at Teri, after he placed a peg and waited for her to say the words knowing the peg would be next. He also gave her another side-eye or two, and she got it. She knew what he was doing. It was amazing: so simple and yet mesmerizing. I am still convinced she has a magic wand somewhere in that bag.

The following day, Cam's occupational therapist, Janet, arrived. She bounced into the house with enough energy to power the entire block. She had fiery red hair cut into a sharp, stylish bob and a smile that nearly reached ear to ear. She was about my age, maybe a year or two older at most, and within minutes, I felt like I had known her all my life. Cam was sitting on the couch with his beloved pillow on his lap, enthralled with his favorite cartoon.

"Hi Cam, I'm Miss Janet."

"Are you watching cartoons, Cam?"

"Oh, is this your pillow Cam?" (I thought, oh no, do not touch the pillow!)

Cam always had his pillow with him. If it wasn't on his lap, it was beside him. If he was venturing into another room, the pillow came with him; waking up and coming downstairs, he would either drag it or pitch it down the stairs depending on his mood. God forbid he would let me carry it down for him. He was, and still is, stingy with his pillow.

Janet put her hand on it, palm up, and I held my breath. Cam, without looking, placed his little dimpled hand in hers. My heart melted. She started to gently put pressure on his forearm, squeezing him slightly from wrist to shoulder. Cam remained focused on the television but did not make any attempt to move away from her. She started to explain to me that kids with autism have sensory needs and that pressure on the joints can provide input and satisfy those needs. I had read several articles about sensory needs by that point, but she was so full of information and so good at explaining it that I felt I learned more from her in an hour than I learned from hours on the internet.

Janet asked me if Cam had any repetitive movements that we noticed. Good lord, "Yes, many," I said. Cam would often dart around the house—not in the way a typical toddler runs around—his path was always very direct and mostly from one corner of the room to the other. He could run full force then stop quickly a half a toe-length away from the wall. He would do this over and over again, and most days nothing seemed to interest him enough to get him to stop, not his favorite toys or turning on a cartoon. I even tried snacks here and there. Sometimes he would choose to run from one corner of the room to the couch where he would slam the top half of his body, including his face, into the cushion. That one was more upsetting to see than the corner-to-corner run because it looked as though he was trying to hurt himself. Again, nothing I tried was enticing enough for him to stop. Some days, I would just have to pick him up and remove him from the room altogether.

He also liked to swing his arm in a circular motion at his side, and at times he would do it so hard you could hear his shoulder crack. Over time we called it *the helicopter*. "Look out, Cam's doing the helicopter." I hope it doesn't sound terrible that we would make light of it. The truth is, if you don't make light of at least some of it, you will go crazy.

I also told Janet about Cam's repetitive vocalizations that were sometimes letter sounds or a combination. One of his favorites was "dikka, dikka, dikka." He did this one all the time, and often, it didn't even seem like he realized he was doing it. He also made a deep humming sound from the back of his throat or his nose. It sounded electronic; that one still comes around sometimes, and it's wild. We still don't understand how he does it! He would also shriek randomly and giggle uncontrollably out of the blue: more behaviors that play a reunion tour every couple of years. She explained that these are forms of vocal self-stimulatory behavior or *vocal stimming*. People with autism use vocal stimming for a number of reasons just as they do with visual stimming, which I touched on a bit earlier, when I thought my son needed an exorcism.

I also told Janet about his need to line items up and how very angry he got if we moved an item out of the line. I told her how Cam folds the towels and how he seems to like sizing things up once he was satisfied with the line or the fold. I watched her face as I spoke, and she did not seem surprised by any of what I was telling her. In fact, sometimes she would jump in and ask questions like, "Do you generally see this behavior at any particular time of the day? Or after an event like going to the grocery store or a family gathering?" She was clearly listening and taking in every detail. When I realized that I had been going on and on, I apologized to her.

She placed her hand on my arm and gave it a squeeze, "Don't be sorry. Your input will make the biggest difference in all of this."

And with that simple statement, Janet gave me the power to help change Cam's prognosis. Janet explained that what I was seeing with Cam were all self-stimulatory behaviors. She continued to explain that children with autism can be over-sensitive to sensory information and that stimming can lessen a sensory overload. On the other side of the coin, some children with autism are under-sensitive to sensory information and those self-stimulatory behaviors can stimulate underactive senses. For Cam, it seems his self-stimulatory behaviors pull from both sides of that coin, which Janet explained can also be common.

When you think about it, we all have self-stimulating behaviors. For example, bouncing our knees, twirling our hair, biting our fingernails or tapping our pens, humming, and whistling. We do this for many reasons: boredom, nervousness, anxiousness, and even exhaustion. The only real difference is that those behaviors are socially acceptable whereas flapping your hands in the air, walking on your tiptoes, or making clicking sounds with your tongue are not. Honestly, I'd rather see masses of people flapping their hands than biting their fingernails. Gross.

I was relieved to reach an understanding of these behaviors, these *stims,* as those of us traveling this winding yellow brick road call them. The vocalizations are vocal stims, the side-eye and sizing up lines of toys are visual stims, and the darting and spinning are vestibular stims. All of which provide input to Cam's central nervous system and, in turn, can help calm him down when he's anxious.

Sometimes he uses them to focus on a task; he even had particular stims at bedtime, mostly spinning in circles that I came to learn—from Janet—that he was doing to stay awake. That little stinker. You see, it's just the same way we tap our pens to stay awake during a less than exciting work meeting or bounce our knees when we are feeling nervous. These are not quirks as many people think; they are, in fact, ways of helping us cope with our surroundings. We all have them.

Over the next several weeks we were seeing progress. Cam became more and more receptive to Teri and Janet, seemingly understanding that they were there for him, and it was time to get to work. At this point, when they came into the house Cam would stop what he was doing and greet them at the door, often trying to help himself to the contents of their bags. We were all fine with it; the acknowledgement was a stepping-stone, although not the politest way to greet a person. We would work on that later. I learned quickly that the therapies were play-based, which made the most sense for Cam's age. Both Teri and Janet were incredible at adjusting and augmenting their treatment plans based on Cam's focus. They each were able to stick to their treatment goals while at the same time kept the sessions fluid and open to Cam's lead. I was so impressed by their ability to turn anything and everything into a teaching moment.

At that time, Gabby was in kindergarten so there were days that she would be at home during sessions, as well as during the summer. They always made sure to include Gabby, making her feel welcome and truly a part of the task at hand. She enjoyed participating and helping out. Cam was thrilled to have her. I realized she was, in fact, a huge asset to the team as she was modeling behavior that would eventually be goals for Cam. For the time being, the focus was keeping him engaged, especially with speech. Teri was so successful in keeping Cam interested that it kept me full of hope. There was always an element of something Cam wanted just out of reach so that he would have to communicate in some way to get it. Moving toward her, reaching, and of course, if he would look her in the eyes, he was granted a puzzle piece: a peg for the board or any number of other items that were needed to finish a task. Teri was consistent in her work with Cam. She never took a day off, was never late, and never augmented the schedule. You could set your watch to Teri—my appreciation for her is endless.

As for occupational therapy, Janet was an expert on self-stimulatory behavior. She taught me different activities to carry out with Cam which is often referred to as a sensory diet. These activities would provide the input Cam was craving and allow him to focus when it was time to get to work. Providing the input for Cam would result in him being better able to stay on task, manage outings, and even go to sleep at night with ease.

As I mentioned on the first day that Janet came, she gently applied pressure on Cam's arms. She would do this at the end of most sessions: arms and legs, paying extra attention to the joints. She explained that joint pressure provides a healthy dose of input. I asked if this was something he was doing by throwing himself onto the couch during darting stims. Cam was not trying to hurt himself at all; he was finding input where he could. She also would have Cam lay inside a blanket. With me on one side and her on the other, we would pick up the ends, make sure he was nice and snug, and swing him back and forth. Cam loved it.

She would do skin brushing, which is brushing the skin along the arms and legs with a natural bristle brush. We would build obstacle courses with couch cushions, pillows, and pop-up tunnels for him to navigate. Simply climbing over pillows and crawling through tunnels provides input and can lessen self-stimulatory behaviors. She would have him jump on a yoga ball while holding his hands as well as lay him across the ball and tip him gently forward and backward while holding onto his ankles.

Most days she would bring an astronaut board, essentially a lazy Susan for kids. She taught me that if I was spinning Cam, I would need to spin him in both directions, equal times. I could spin him on his back, belly, and laying on each side to provide equal and unique input. This was Cam's favorite, and he would light up when he saw Janet bringing it into the house. He was so in love with it that after the first few times, Janet no longer had to say, "Turn on to your belly Cam." He would switch to each position the second she stopped spinning him and shoot her a little grin as if to say, *I am ready.*

While doing these activities with Cam, Janet would work on different skills. In between physical activities, he would sit still and stay on task, whether it was practicing fastening buttons or pulling up zippers, peeling a banana, or using a fork. It was amazing to see him stay on task for periods of time up to twenty minutes. I turned into a sponge during their sessions. I always stayed in the room with both Teri and Janet so I could learn from them; the only times I would leave would be if I seemed to be a distraction for Cam. I mimicked Teri's labeling when playing with Cam and carried out the sensory diet set forth by Janet twice a day at minimum. Over time, my relationship with Cam became more reciprocal. He was more present, and even though he was still not using words to communicate, we were in sync. It was magical.

Everything I learned I would share with Justin, and he too would follow through. And Gabby, well she was probably the most diligent with it. As a matter of fact, one afternoon I had Cam standing on the yoga ball while using my knee to keep it wedged between me and the couch. I was holding his hands, and he was jumping.

Gabby, seven years old at the time, walked in and started singing "Cam is jumping, Cam is jumping, on the ball, on the ball" to the rhythm of "Frère Jacques."

Cam squealed and jumped harder; then Gabby switched it up and sang "Cam is marching, Cam is marching, on the ball, on the ball," and with that, Cam switched from jumping to marching. I was in awe of both of them. She was labeling our actions just as she had watched both Teri and Janet doing in their sessions. Because they always included Gabby, if she was around and willing, she seemed like a little intern, even making suggestions at times. Teri and Janet would follow her lead. Once we were finished with our jumping time, I gave Gabby a turn on the yoga ball. I held onto her hands, and we sang the song with her name in it this time. She was having a blast and Cam danced around us giggling and clapping. I will never forget that moment.

As the weeks turned into months, I would be lying if I said I was not getting anxious to hear words from Cam. At one point during those first few months, I noticed the therapists starting to use the sign language sign for the word "more." When they asked Cam if he wanted more of something, they would use the sign and sometimes, hand over hand, show Cam how to make the sign. As with most things, Cam caught on quickly and was copying the sign. I had mixed emotions: did this mean full-on sign language was on the horizon? I was happy to see him use it, but at the same time, I didn't want him to. I wanted him to speak. I just could not let that go, and of course, I wasn't the only one.

Cam and I used to take Gabby to school in the mornings and pick her up each afternoon. One of her classmates had a little sister the same age as Cam. The little girl loved Gabby, and every time she would see her in the parking lot at drop off and pick up, she would run to her with her arms outstretched and yell, "Gabby, Gabby, Gabby."

One day as we were driving home, Gabby said, "Do you think Cam will ever do that?"

I said, "Do what?"

She said, "Call my name."

My heart sank. I spent many nights awake, wondering if I would ever hear him call out *mom*. I didn't even think to wonder if Gabby had the same wish.

I said to her, "We are going to do our best to get him there."

That night, I was on the phone with my aunt, and I told her that the team was starting to teach him sign language.

She said, "Why the hell are they doing that? Teach him how to talk!"

The saying is *out of the mouths of babes,* but in this case, I'm going with *out of the mouths of septuagenarians.* I would need to ask Teri and Janet to forgo the sign language, at least for a bit longer. We were seeing so much progress, and Cam understood the importance of communicating and the outcomes. He was starting to use different gestures, pointing, or grabbing our hands, and taking us to something he wanted. We were even seeing some eye contact that seemed to have purpose. There had to be a way to transition his physical mode of communication into speech. I didn't know how to ask them to stop; they were the professionals after all. They had years of experience between them, and I had only months. I didn't want them to think I was being disrespectful or that I had unrealistic expectations but decided there was no easy way to broach the subject other than just coming right out and saying it.

"I don't want you to use sign language with him yet."

Thankfully, both Janet and Teri were receptive to it. They understood where I was coming from, but both did, in their own way, try to make sure I understood that sign language could be in Cam's future. I don't think they were placating me in agreeing to nix the sign language or buying time; I think they were inspired by Cam's progress and maybe—just maybe—also wanted to prove that doctor wrong.

Often, Teri would still be at the house when Janet arrived, and when time allowed, the two would compare notes and collaborate. Between all of us, we targeted Cam's motivations: praise was number one (the kid was a ham) and a prize was number two. It didn't even have to be a new toy; it could be an extra five minutes with Teri's peg board or a second go in the blanket swing as the reward. Last, but certainly not least, was a treat. Any snack would do—what kid doesn't love a good snack?

Cam's eye contact was still lacking quite a bit, but we all used it as something to reward. If he would look at any of us in the eye, we would reward him with one of the three motivators. Around this same time, I had been reading about orbital swings while looking up all things sensory input related. Orbital swings are widely used in therapy and can be a great addition to sensory diets. The swings found in therapy rooms look like a saucer and are typically hung from a large frame. I knew I wanted one for Cam, but unfortunately, space in my house was limited, and they are expensive. So instead, I purchased a sack swing for 40 bucks. They hang from a single rope and therefore are ... orbital. I hung that swing as close to the middle of my living room as possible. It hung from the joist Justin found closest to the middle.

I bought the swing with the intent of using it as sensory input, but shortly after the swing was in place, I thought that maybe I could also use it to bring out more communication from Cam. One morning, I put Cam in the swing then sat on the floor in front of him. I waited. He was scanning the room, eyes moving from corner to corner then floor to ceiling, and so on. As he was doing this, what I hoped would happen, happened. His scan brought his eyes to mine, and in that instant, I swung that little shit ... hard! He screamed with delight, giggling, and kicking his feet. I swung him for a bit as we laughed and cheered, then I stopped the swing. I sat back down on the floor and waited again. Lo and behold, after several seconds, his scan brought us eye to eye again. *Whoosh,* I pushed the swing. He shrieked and laughed, and as the swing came back toward me, he reached out and swiped his hand over my cheek, keeping eye contact with me. It was just a few seconds, but it felt so important.

After sharing the experience with his dad, his sister, and the team, everyone was on board. Within days, Cam knew he wasn't getting anywhere in that swing until he locked eyes with us. From that point on, the second he got in the swing he would, with all the intention in the world, look into my eyes. Once it was clear Cam understood that looking into my eyes would result in a big push, I stopped wondering *if* he would ever talk and started to wonder *when.* I was convinced we could get there by building on the understanding Cam achieved in that 40-dollar swing that looked like a giant scrotum hanging in the middle of my living room.

By this point we were several months in, and Camden was making great strides in many areas. We had gained a true understanding of his self-stimulatory behaviors and were able to provide input through the sensory diet, and in turn, we were seeing less and less stims. His on-task focus was getting stronger by the day. His self-help skills, everything from using a fork correctly to slipping on his slide on shoes, were coming along. Our routine of school drop-off, therapy sessions, school pick up, afternoon sensory diet, dinner, and evening sensory diet now felt second nature. One evening while everyone was winding down in the living room, I sat down next to Cam on the couch with part of my leg on his pillow.

"Ho," he said with a bit of an attitude and pulled the pillow out from under me.

"Did he just call his pillow *HO*?" I laughed.

All three of us were on our feet while Cam sat on the couch looking at us.

Justin said, "Is that your ho Cam?"

Cam replied "ho" with a loud silly voice and hugged his pillow.

He was grinning ear to ear and looking at all of us waiting for our next reaction. Gabby was yelling, "Oh my god, oh my god, oh my god," and jumping up and down.

I was laughing hysterically. I repeated Justin's question, "Cam, is that your ho?" And again, Cam replied, "ho" but with even more gusto and threw his pillow up in the air.

Justin said, "Don't throw your ho Cam!"

At this point I was crying, laughing, and yelling, "That is a word. *That is a word*!"

Justin threw his arms around me in a giant bear hug, Gabby was holding on to our legs, and Cam joined the celebration by jumping up and down on the couch chanting, "ho, ho, ho, ho!"

I snatched him up. He was still gripping the pillow as I swung him around "You love your ho, Cam!"

We were so excited to hear him speak, but we also saw just how funny this was ... Cam's ho! Of course, Gabby was too young to get the joke, but it just added to the whole event. I wish there was a word in the English language, or any language for that matter, to describe how I felt. As you can imagine, the *ho* joke is still going strong.

For years, "No Cam, you can't take your ho to the museum."

"Cam! Don't drag your ho down the stairs."

"Don't leave your ho on the floor, buddy."

"Cam, come get your ho."

And so on. As a matter of fact, I walked past Cam's room just the other day and he was balancing four pillows on top of his head.

I yelled out, "That's a lot of hos on your head!"

Gabby, now 18, gets the joke, and Justin erupted in laughter. Cam just shook his head and thought we were crazy.

After we settled down from Cam's first *ho* celebration, I sent a text message to both Teri and Janet. There was no way in hell I was waiting until their next visits to share the news. Over the next few months, we started to hear other labels, "al" for ball and "ish" for those little fish crackers all kids love. It was truly like a flood gate had opened. Cam had already learned that certain actions would gain results in terms of wants and needs but once the *ho* came out, it seemed to click for him, so the labels just kept coming. None of us cared that they were not true words yet because we knew it was a start. It took everything in me not to call that doctor from almost a year prior and tell her to get bent.

Building Puzzles Under Water

The More the Merrier

Cam's third birthday was quickly approaching, and I was faced with the fact that the early intervention program ends at age three. Cam would no longer receive services through the county because he could enter an area preschool. The simple fact was, he was not ready for that. I'm embarrassed to say that I did not have a plan; I had no idea what to do next. I was so focused on each day as it happened that I didn't plan for the future. Typically, at this stage parents of children around three years old have very broad and fluid goals for their kids: pre-school is a given, and they may start to think of little league or dance classes, maybe even a summer day camp program. But upon an autism diagnosis, the goals become so exact. How can you dream about T-ball when you're still teaching your son to recognize when another person enters a room, much less a ball coming at him in the outfield? In my mind, *what's next* would come after we accomplished some of these immediate goals. I didn't stop to consider that the immediate goals could take months and even years.

Thankfully, by this time Teri and Janet were truly part of my family. They were helping us raise my son after all. Because of this, I was not embarrassed to tell them I did not know what to do next. On a day that their schedules overlapped, I simply said, "What do I do now?" and "Please don't leave me!" half joking, half serious as a heart attack— something else my mum used to say. I was so scared to be without them.

55

They explained that Cam could receive wraparound services, and that he didn't have to go to preschool to receive them. They went on to explain that I could have in-home wraparound services at any time, even prior to the age of three. That was news to me. I didn't know much about wraparound services, but I had always thought that it was an in-school service only. So, true to form, that night Justin and I took to the Internet to research wraparound service providers in the area. We didn't want to add more hours of therapy to Cam's schedule. He was already receiving a good bit, but we did think it was a good idea to overlap a bit. Teri and Janet had such a strong understanding of Cam that it only made sense that a new person should work alongside them, if possible.

After our online research and receiving referrals from other families, Justin and I decided on a wraparound service provider that also had in-house psychologists. At this point we still had not replaced the doctor that diagnosed Cam. Let's just say that the animosity lingered, but at least we knew what we were *not* looking for in a new doctor.

I made the call, and the person I spoke with over the phone was extremely patient and explained how their process worked. Cam would go into the office for an evaluation with one of the doctors who would then recommend treatment, and a behavior specialist consultant, or BSC, would be assigned. Whether you have been a part of the autism community for a while or just starting out, you know there are countless acronyms. I will do my best to keep it to a minimum. Once assigned, the

BSC would visit us in our home. Their role is to write the treatment plans to be carried out by the therapeutic support staff, or TSS. These are the folks you will see most often. The BSC visits periodically to observe treatment, evaluate, adjust, and add to the plan when needed.

The first appointment was set, and I was surprised by how unfazed I was. We had the diagnosis and several months of therapies under our belts. We were seeing steady progress and understood Cam and his personal brand of autism more and more each day. The way I saw it, this appointment was for me to interview the doctor. I knew I wanted someone I could tell was listening, I knew I wanted someone who would look at Cam as an individual and not use a blanket of general information about autism to label him. Essentially, I wanted a doctor to see Cam first, autism second, and I would not settle for anything less. Justin couldn't make the appointment due to his work schedule. We discussed whether to choose a new date or if Cam and I would go alone on this one. In the end, we decided to keep the appointment. Justin and I have always been on the exact same page when it comes to raising our children, so it was no surprise to me that we agreed to keep the momentum going.

When Cam and I entered the office, we were greeted by a very sweet older lady who asked us to sign in and have a seat. She said *hello* to Cam but did not wait for a response from him. She got right back to work on her computer. You can't beat the comfort of knowing you are among people who *get it*. So far so good. Cam was in a great mood; he immediately started to play with the wooden puzzles in the waiting room, completely at ease.

The door opened and a very tall man in a white jacket with a head of billowy white hair called Cam's name, and Cam actually looked up from his puzzle! I think it was because the doctor's voice was quite deep, and I think this intrigued Cam. We followed him down the hall and into his office, he was whistling and had a bit of a bounce to his step. In the doorway of his office, he shook my hand and gave a quick tousle of Cam's hair, "Welcome," he said. "What a pleasure to meet with the two of you today."

He had toys in his office, and Cam made a beeline for the play barn with animals. I sat in the chair opposite of the doctor's desk and took quick note of a few drawings he had posted behind him: patient artwork, wonderful. Although the doctor was quite tall and with that deep intimidating voice, his manner was very calm and very patient. The first thing he said was, "Tell me a bit about Cam. What does he like to do? What are his favorite toys and activities?" This is how this type of appointment should start. I told him that Cam loved puzzles and was very good at them; that he loved to swing and to ride on his push bike; that he loved music; and he loved any cartoons that included music and singing. He loved to build blocks and play with cars and bouncy balls were also a favorite go to.

He said, "Well, these are all wonderful things," and with that, he swiveled in his chair and took a small gong off the shelf behind him.

Cam was next to him at a table where the toys were, and he said Cam's name, but Cam didn't turn around. So, the doctor gently tapped Cam on the shoulder and bent down closer to eye level, and Cam turned toward him. He placed the gong on his desk and pushed it toward Cam then gave it a little tap with the mallet. Cam's eyes got huge, and he leapt forward.

The doctor then handed the mallet to Cam and said, "You try."

With that, Cam struck the gong hard and let out a squeal as it sounded, and it tipped over. I thought, *oh shit. He is going to break that, and we are gonna get the boot.* But the doctor simply caught it in time and let out a bit of a giggle. He and Cam continued to take turns as he started to ask questions that mirrored the parent questionnaire we had completed twice before. At no point did he try to force any eye contact with Cam or look for reciprocal behavior for that matter.

To my delight, Cam would take a turn tapping the gong then hand the mallet back for the doctor to take his turn. Did I think the doctor was taking notes in his head? Absolutely. Did I think he was looking at Cam as a child first? Absolutely. Was I fighting back tears? Absolutely.

For the next six years, he and Cam would play with the gong at every appointment. We will call him Dr. T. from here on out. I had completed a third questionnaire as he and Cam did their thing, answered more questions, and signed some additional paperwork. When I looked up, he and Cam were playing with a cast iron train engine. Dr. T. had taken it down from his shelf. Again, I was worried Cam would send it sailing off the edge of the desk, but instead, he played with it carefully. The doctor explained that it was a gift from another patient that he had kept on his shelf for many years. His patient loved to talk about trains, and Dr. T. said they would discuss trains every time they met. I handed him the questionnaire, and he placed it at the side of his desk. He said, "I can tell this guy is ready for big things. You will have to push him, but I have a feeling you are up to the task."

He said that he believed Cam would benefit greatly from a form of therapy referred to as ABA therapy. ABA stands for Applied Behavior Analysis, which is centered on the understanding of how behavior works in real situations. In a nutshell, the goal of this type of therapy is to decrease behaviors that are a hindrance to communication, learning, and social skills. Before taking our leave, about an hour and a half later, he thanked me for allowing him to meet Cam. What a great thing to say.

"One more thing," Dr. T. said as he opened his desk drawer.

He pulled out a small plastic container full of M&M's and shook the container. He asked if Cam could have some. Little did he know those were, and remain, Cam's favorite treat.

I said, "Yes, of course" and he shook the container again and nudged Cam's shoulder.

Cam turned around and Dr. T. removed the lid. Cam started to jump up and down, his eyes round as saucers. Dr. T. said "just a few" with his finger in the air. Cam had another plan and proceeded to take an entire handful and shove them all into his mouth at once.

Dr. T.'s face lit up and with a boisterous laugh he said, "Man after my own heart."

Cam and I were sold. I drove home wishing Justin could have been there, if for nothing else but to replace his past experience with the first doctor. I arrived at the appointment guarded and leery; I left on cloud nine.

I was excited to fill Justin in on all things Dr. T. when he got home from work that evening. I think I was talking a mile a minute. I gave him as much detail as I could, so he felt in the loop. I know he felt bad not being able to go and it was hard on him receiving most of the information second hand. I was the one at home with Cam while he worked his butt off making sure I could stay at home to accommodate the therapy hours. I'm not sure he will never know how much I admire him for the sacrifices he made. That night, we sat side by side at the computer searching for information on ABA therapy. It did truly seem like a perfect fit for Cam.

Within a week, I received a call, and Cam was prescribed 20 hours per week of in-home therapy. Both Justin and I were a bit shocked by the number of hours. I mean, we didn't know what to expect, but it seemed like a lot—like, a lot a lot. With all the progress we were seeing we just were not expecting that. Looking back, I'm pretty sure we thought Cam was not going to need much more; it's as though we thought once he started talking it would be smooth sailing. Clearly, we were still so new at the game.

Next on the agenda was a visit from the BSC who was assigned to Cam. When he arrived, he was very upbeat and excited to meet with us. He had a red and white striped polo shirt on that reminded me of the popular search and find books. He even had the black rimmed glasses. I liked him immediately. He presented a broad definition of ABA therapy so as not to overwhelm me, it seemed, which I appreciated. I am the type of person who retains information by doing, not necessarily by listening. Being a hands-on-kind-of-gal, I was satisfied that I understood the outline and would watch and learn the subtext during the sessions, just as I had with the early intervention team.

When we started to discuss the schedule, I was hesitant about four-hour sessions five days a week. First of all, what toddler will stay engaged that long? Secondly, when would Cam have time to be, well … Cam? And third, how would this affect our family as a unit? In particular, how would Gabby feel, especially over the summer months when she was used to us going out and about?

I felt like an asshole. Here is this amazing opportunity and I thought it was too much. How could I feel that any help for Cam would be too much help? It felt selfish, but my gut told me that the time outside of therapy was just as important, so I asked if we could choose less hours. Did I just look a gift horse in the mouth?

To my surprise, the BSC was completely open and understanding of my fears. He said we could choose any amount of time and that I did not have to decide that minute. He also said that we could add and subtract hours at any time and assured me that not all the hours had to be in our home. We could certainly visit parks, play centers, and even the local swimming pool with Cam's TSS. This type of therapy follows the child and is often fluid, centering on real-time social interactions. He also mentioned that because siblings are typically the best teachers, the TSS would involve Gabby in any way she and I were comfortable with. If at any point she wanted to join in, she was welcome.

I was really happy with his response and willingness to work with us to find the right balance. He then took to the floor to play with Cam. At the time, Cam was playing with a small racetrack and cars, but he was ignoring the track and lining the cars up beside it. The BSC asked Cam if he could play with a car and Cam looked up at him and pushed one in his direction. The BSC could not have known how hard we had worked to get him to that point. Before his early intervention team worked their magic, that never would have happened. The BSC took the car and said *thank you* to Cam. He ran it around the racetrack but then immediately placed it back in Cam's line. He asked Cam for another car, and again, Cam pushed one toward him. He ran the second car over the racetrack then again placed it back in Cam's line. I was impressed; he was showing Cam the appropriate way of playing with the set but also honoring his need to line the cars up, and Cam was tolerating it. Not only was he tolerating it, but he began to mirror the BSC's actions running a car along the track and then placing it back in his beloved line.

The initial visit with the BSC was about two hours. He played with Cam for most of it while asking me various questions and explaining the types of goals that are set and why. Toward the end of his visit, he explained that he felt as though he had a great TSS match for Cam. Since the TSS is the person responsible for fulfilling the hours and treatment plan, I was eager to hear more. He told me that his name was Zach, he was fairly new to the game, but he was full of ideas and excitement. He also disclosed that Zach was his younger brother. I am always open to folks who are fresh out of school or training; they tend to seem more present, more open, and excited about their craft. I also thought if he was anything like his brother—loud and animated (I say that with admiration)—Cam would love him. I had no issue with his newness or his relation to our BSC. I brought up my hopes of overlapping wraparound services and early intervention so they could work as a team until Cam turned three. He was thrilled and thought that Teri's and Janet's input would be beyond advantageous for both him and Zach. In fact, he was so thrilled, he threw me a double high five and then seemed to be embarrassed by it immediately. I was fine with it; I felt like I was building the A-Team, and what A-team doesn't double high five?

That evening, Justin and I discussed the appointment, and he was in complete agreement with me on all points, most importantly the number of hours per week. He too had the same concerns but did not seem to feel guilty over it the way that I did. Justin is a very cut and dry person which helped me to get over feeling selfish and feel more empowered. We decided to take it down to 15 hours per week and see how it went, which was key in all of this for me. The diagnosis, the doctors and therapists, the gobs of information on the internet; it is all so overwhelming, not to mention the endless paperwork. You have to find your ground, or you will lose your footing.

That night we also addressed the elephant in the room: how to manage the logistics of Cam's schedule as a two-income household. I had been working in real estate for close to 13 years. I was able to create an adapted schedule to be at home with Cam and accommodate his early intervention visits twice a week. I loved my career, and I was good at it, but to be good at you had to be available. The new therapy schedule was not going to allow that. I knew it, and Justin knew it too. How would we survive? Justin being Justin was cool as could be saying, "We will figure it out."

The first thing we did was sell my car to get rid of the payment. We then canceled our cable and proceeded to shave off other expenses by choosing cheaper packages and canceling various subscriptions. There were no take out dinners or Friday night pizza parties anymore, and random shopping sprees for frivolous things were out for the next several years. We examined and adjusted just about every expense other than Gabby's extracurricular activities, which we left in place.

Often Justin's mother, Cindy, and my sister, Maura, stepped in and helped us keep her little life as normal as possible. Maura would regularly take Gabby on outings to places like the museum and local festivals and do things we certainly did not have the extra money for.

We became dollar store shoppers and coupon clippers and only purchased necessities. Holiday and birthday gifts were often monetarily supported by Justin's mom, and she never hesitated to help us. Anytime I tried to protest, she would simply say, "Those are my grandkids." I had lost my own mum at the age of 24 and had always been self-sufficient. I was not used to the help, but Cindy never made us feel as though we owed her anything. She was, and still is, very giving. Both Cindy and my sister have been supportive in many ways, always accepting Cam for exactly who he is, and Cam has a wonderful relationship with both of them.

Several months in, Justin decided to take a second job. A few days a week he would come home from work, have dinner, get a few hours in with the kids, sleep for an hour or two, and then head back out to a night shift stocking grocery shelves. Our only other option would have been to shorten therapy hours so I could find a part time job, but then Cam would have to go to daycare, and any money I made would need to pay for that. I worried endlessly about Justin working like he did—on almost no sleep—but he was completely against me working a night shift and insisted he would be OK. There was nothing easy about that time in our lives, but Justin was right: we, along with the help of our family, did in fact make it work.

Building Puzzles Under Water

The A-Team

Wrap around services were set to begin on a Monday, and that morning Cam was a bit out of sorts. It was around this time that we started noticing his sleep patterns drastically changed. He was waking up between 12 a.m. and 2 a.m. and staying awake sometimes until the sun came up. He was simply wide awake and would play in his crib. He never tried to alert us that he was awake, nor did he cry or fuss; he was just awake. This is very common for children on the spectrum, but as a parent, it is hell on earth.

We tried everything from a new evening sensory diet to no screens, including the TV, an hour before bedtime; a white noise machine; Epsom salt baths; a banana before bed; a weighted blanket. Just about everything we read or that was recommended to us we tried, but nothing worked. Because of this, we would see an uptick in self-stimulatory behaviors. It seemed that he would try on all his stims in order to make it through the day. He never actually seemed tired, just extra stimmy and, in turn, unfocused and hard to reach.

The night before wraparound services started, he had been up since 2 a.m. so by the time his appointment came around, he was *stimtastic*, as we call it in our house. I decided to have him ride his push bike around the back yard, something that he loved to do, and also provided a lot of sensory input for him. He was happily creating crop circles in the grass by 9 a.m. and belting out his version of the song "Firework." I couldn't help but sing along with him "boom, boom, boom," anything to keep myself awake. I heard Zach's car pull onto our driveway, and I opened the back gate and waved hello with a motion to come on back. Zach bounced through the gate, and before Cam was in his line of vision, he heard the catchy song and started to sing along.

He is quite tall, dark brown hair, and big brown eyes. He was in his early twenties but looked like a teenager. His voice bellowed as he introduced himself, and he nearly crushed my hand with his handshake. Yep, he was going to fit right in.

He told me he was very excited to work with Cam and that his brother had so many great things to say about him and our family. He headed toward Cam, "Wow, I like your bike buddy! Can I give you a push?" Cam was moving at a pretty good pace but looked in Zach's direction as he rounded one of his grass tracks. Zach bent down, grabbed the back handle, and started pushing Cam along.

My phone rang, not the best timing, but I had to take it. I had been waiting to hear back from the children's hospital in our area to get Cam into on-site speech and occupational therapy since wraparound would be primarily focused on the ABA therapy. As I was talking, I turned to see that Zach had pushed Cam up the slanted part of the yard, and I thought *No. He is not going to let go of the bike, is he?* Sure enough, Zach let go of the push bike and sent Cam sailing down the hill! I threw my phone and bolted toward

Cam yelling, "He won't be able to stop himself!" Remember, Cam was just under three years old.

Zach started running down the hill, his face beet red. Cam made it almost to the bottom where the yard levels off. I'll never forget his face: he had a giant smile, but his eyes looked wild, part fear and part adrenaline. His sandy blond hair, blown back with the wind.

I got to him just in time. I lifted him off the bike, and the bike hit the level yard and did a triple lindy, bouncing up and spinning in the air. Cam was howling with laughter and screaming, "More, more!" This quickly became one of his newest and most favorite words.

The kid just had the ride of his life. I couldn't help but laugh, while Zach apologized over and over again with his hands over his mouth, just wrecked with total embarrassment. "It's OK, he's OK!" I set Cam down and continued to reassure Zach. I felt so bad for him; I can't imagine how he felt. "No harm, no foul," I said as I patted him on the shoulder and then realized Cam had grabbed the push bike and was trying to make his way back up the hill. Zach turned and ran toward him, "Oh no buddy, let's not do that again!" He scooped him up and started spinning him in the air. Cam spread his arms and legs and started to sing his version of his favorite pop song again, "Ah, ah, ah. Boom, boom, boom."

Cam was sold. He loved Zach from day one. Zach and I both joined in on the remix for a minute before I suggested we head into the house, Zach seemed relieved by the idea.

Armed with the treatment plan his brother had written, Zach was ready to roll. He was exuberant and fun and seemed to have an endless supply of energy. He seemed to become a part of our family immediately.

For the next two weeks, they would begin work on staying on task using short exercises with play in between. Zach had a very good understanding of self-stimulatory behaviors, aside from witnessing many of Cams in those first few days. I filled him in on some others and walked him through the sensory diet Janet had laid out. His time would overlap with Janet and Teri's time by a half hour each week. They loved Zach immediately. He was always positive and willing to learn. He took in everything they told him about their time with Cam, and he applied the information to his sessions with ease. This really was the A-Team.

Toward the end of the first two weeks, Zach had told me that his brother had moved up in the company and a new BSC would be assigned. I won't lie, I was a little upset. Here we were two weeks in, and already changes were being made. I had heard many horror stories about the high turnover of TSS and BSC roles—families never knowing who was coming, no one staying long enough to make a difference. I did my best to stay positive, and I am sure Zach was a bit worried himself. On the third week the new BSC came for observation, and Zach and I filled her in on all things Cam. She seemed hesitant around Cam. Because he was not always engaged, she seemed a bit lost. He did not acknowledge her at any time during her visit. She was as kind as could be: very soft spoken and seemed to be a patient person. She mentioned that she generally worked with kids with attention-deficit/hyperactivity disorder (ADHD) but had some experience with kids on the spectrum. Zach and I gave each other a quick side eye.

After she left, I said, "Let's see how the next visit goes." Zach agreed, but I could tell he was concerned too. That night, when Justin got home, I told him about the visit. He was not thrilled. It didn't make sense to either of us—why would they send someone who specializes in ADHD? Justin also agreed that we would see how the next visit played out, but we were not going to waste much time if things did not start to jive.

Cam's progress was moving right along. He was gaining more words, or more of his brand of words, I should say. Many did not come out fully formed, but he used them consistently, and they were darn close. I'd say, in all, he had close to ten. The favorites were "ho" (I can't help it. I still laugh at this.), "more" (sometimes he would even pull out the sign for *more* as he said it), "out" (which he typically used in the mornings when he wanted rescued from his crib), and "swing" (which often came out as "ing"). For the most part, his first words were that of action. He was learning how to communicate his needs vocally through our consistent use of labeling action and then taking action. We would walk into his bedroom and say "out" then immediately take him out of his crib, and over time, he would repeat the word. Instead of waiting for eye contact when we sat him in the swing, which had become automatic for Cam, we would say "swing" and then push the swing right away.

We labeled everything all the time. Eventually, once he would start repeating the word, or at least something very close to it, we would move to saying, "What do you want, Cam?" and he would say the word on his own. Everyone would repeat the correct words back to him when he would use shortened versions, but often, he seemed to just like the way he said things better. We all let it slide at times because he was already leaps and bounds away from his original diagnosis ... plus he was a charmer. The kid knew how to work a crowd and may or may not have had all of us wrapped around his little finger. He would say his words with a little tilt of the head, or he would put his hands on his cheeks, sometimes he would grab onto your hand and look up at you with a sweet smile to get what he wanted. He knew what he was doing.

Zach continued to work with him to stay on task. It was slow going, but Zach was patient and consistent, which is key. By this time, school was out for the summer, and Gabby was back to being the little intern. She often chose to be a part of their day—Zach was great at including her. Gabby has always been very intuitive, and because of this, she very naturally understood the therapies. You could see it in her everyday interactions with Cam. He loved to be around her, and he followed her everywhere.

I started to notice that every time they went up or down the steps together, Gabby would count the steps. The team was only starting to approach letters and numbers; we were more focused on sensory needs and time on task. Not Gab though: one night at bedtime, we were all heading up the stairs, and out of the clear blue, Cam, standing near the top of the stairs, started counting "one, oo, teeee!" Justin and I just looked at each other in shock. Gabby joined in the count, and Justin threw his arms up in the air and said, "OK then, I guess Gab taught Cam how to count." We broke into laughter and Gabby was beaming, so proud of herself and of Cam. Justin and I were in awe of both of them.

The four of us stayed up much too late that night just counting and giggling away. A few days later, Gabby was in the bath, and I had gone into the bathroom to check the water level. Apparently, she had added more bubble solution when I left, so now, she was engulfed in a good two feet of bubbles. "Holy smokes, kid!" She was laughing hysterically, and Cam toddled in to see what the commotion was all about.

He started jumping and squealing, and Gab grabbed a handful of bubbles and blew them onto Cam's head; he looked like a little gnome. Gabby said, "Bubbles, Cam?" and he started jumping again and making little chirping noises. Again, she said, "Bubbles?" and blew more his way. They landed on his face this time, and he wiped them away. He shook them off his hands laughing.

"Bubbles," Gabby said in a high-pitched voice. He waved his little arms in a give-me-more sort of motion, but this time Gab did not oblige him. She waited, and when he started to protest with his mad face and some mean grunts, she said it again, "Bubbles? Bubbles, Cam?" He tried to form the word, and I was holding my breath. At this point, that would be the first two-syllable word for him. He let out a "bub!" Gabby said, "Almost Cam, *bubbles*?" She was not going to budge.

His little eyebrows pulled together—he looked so serious—then it happened ... the sweetest two syllables came out of his mouth, "bub-bles!" he yelled with his fists in the air. You could tell he was delighted with himself. Gabby and I were screaming, "He said it! He said it!" Our reaction was fuel for Cam. Over and over, "bubbles, bubbles," he chanted. I grabbed my phone and started recording for Justin. You can hear Gabby's voice say, "What do you want Cam?" and on camera and in extreme close up, as our bathroom was very small, you see Cam with his chubby little cheeks belting out "bubbles" over and over.

I was walking on sunshine. The groove was there; the progress was happening. Nothing could stop us. Aside from his growing vocabulary, Cam was developing quite the little personality. He loved to play jokes and be silly. Sometimes, he would sidle up beside you and give you a sweet look, seemingly about to feed you a fish cracker, and as he brought it close to your face, he would pull it away and gobble it up. If he was watching a favorite show and something funny would happen, he would look at you and then slap his knee, "funny" he would say and point at the TV. He even started to do little magic tricks. He would place a tea towel over a small toy then pick it up, toy and all, then gasp with wide eyes as if to say *look, it disappeared!*

He was also starting to show concern for others. If Gabby was upset, he would go to her and sort of size her up, looking back at me as if to say, *Are you gonna fix this?* Or if something sad was happening on one of his favorite shows, he would pat us on the knee as if to soothe us. In just under a year and half, he was more present and more engaged, and even though I was starting to grasp the fact that there would always be mountains to climb, I was allowing myself time to sit in wonder of it all.

The week came for the BSC's second visit, and Zach and I found ourselves having to explain what sensory needs are, self-stimulatory behaviors, and sensory diets for most of her visit. To work with Cam, knowledge of these things is essential. She continued to be very apprehensive around Cam for the remainder of her time. He was disengaged and disinterested. When she left, I looked at Zach and said, "She has to go." There was no way she could write effective treatment plans for him with her background. I am absolutely sure she was a wonderful BSC for children with ADHD, but she just was not the right fit for Cam.

I called the office and spoke with the scheduling coordinator. I told the gentleman that the current BSC, as lovely as she was, did not have the background needed to be an effective part of the team and that Cam needed someone who specialized in spectrum disorder. Assigning anyone else without the right qualifications would be an additional waste of everyone's time. I was polite but direct, leaving no room for negotiation. When I got off the phone, Zach said, "I hope they give Cam Radhika." A few days later

I received a call; Cam's case had indeed been assigned to Zach's pick.

I believe that whoever coined the phrase *a force of nature* did so after meeting Radhika. Where do I even begin? She arrived the following week. I opened the door to a tiny little thing with beautiful, long dark hair and intense dark eyes. She walked in with her flip flops and brightly colored quilted bag. She was cheerful in her greeting and immediately flipped off her shoes and took her place on the floor next to Cam who was already in the middle of a task with Zach. Zach had a lot of great things to say about Radhika in the days leading up to her first visit, so I was very excited to meet her and tell her all about Cam's successes thus far. She told Zach to continue with what he was working on, and that she would observe and talk with me in the meantime.

At the end of the session, Radhika said she had read all of Zach's daily notes from the beginning, as well as Cam's treatment plan and intake notes from Dr. T. She said she was very impressed, but—let me lay this out for you now— Radhika is not one to let folks rest on their laurels. She will applaud progress but then immediately raise the bar, fully expecting everyone involved to get to work. Usually, once the accolades were spoken, the next word was *but*. She said, "Everything in your house is too available to Cam. You make everything too easy for him." Whoa, don't hold back! She went on to point out that he had complete access to all his toys, pillows, and other comfort items. Snacks were an effortless grab from the pantry or a juice box from the fridge. She even mentioned that I peeled his banana for him at snack time. Because everything in his environment was so accessible, we were not giving him enough opportunity to communicate his wants and needs.

Radhika did reiterate how impressed she was, and she was particularly complimentary about our use of the swing. She was very excited about how involved our entire family was, *but*—there it is again—we could be doing more. She said we would need to be OK with some discomfort, both for Cam and ourselves, as it was time to push a bit harder. She said very intently, "He can handle it."

We did tiptoe around his moods a lot, but it was to get the most out of him when he was engaged. We did not realize that we were likely creating a world where Cam would only have to comply if he felt like it. I was a bit deflated after she left. In truth, though, we were getting too comfortable with his status at the time. Radhika thought five to 10 words was great, but it also meant that 10 to 20 words should be the goal now. The bottom line was, we needed Radhika and her cheerful little quilted bag filled with large demands.

Justin and I got to work trying to make Cam's environment a bit harder to maneuver on his own. We filled a mesh laundry bag with all his beloved bouncy balls and hung it from the ceiling in the corner of the living room. The child locks went back on the snack cabinet and all his toys were placed behind locked doors. True to form, Cam quickly figured out how to open the child locks—the little shit—but we were still able to make his environment a bit more difficult to navigate. There was certainly some frustration, which at times, would turn into full-on tantrums. It was not easy for us to wait out the meltdowns, but soon when he wanted to play with the bouncy balls, he would stand under the mesh bag. We would then say "ball" and bring the bag down for him.

Snacks and drinks were out of his reach now, so he would stand in front of the refrigerator or the cabinet, and again, we would say "drink" or "snack." "What do you want, Cam, a snack?" Handing him the unpeeled bananas seemed to annoy Cam the most. He didn't get upset, but he would look at us like, "You think this is funny?" We used the word *open* with the bananas since it could be utilized in more situations versus the word peel. Lo and behold, over the next few weeks he started to add these words to his vocabulary, understanding that verbalization would grant him the object he was interested in just as he learned that looking into my eyes while sitting in the living room swing meant he would get a big push.

We were all surprised by how quickly his vocabulary grew—all except for Radhika—she knew it wouldn't take long. We continued to celebrate every word like it was his first: cheering and clapping every time he spoke. Cam would get so excited and bounce up and down repeating the word with a huge smile on his face. He was proud of himself, and it was amazing to watch. Somewhere in there, Justin, Gabby, and I fully let go of the question, *Will he ever talk?* And we never looked back. That bar, the one Radhika would not let us leave in place once a goal was achieved, was constantly raised. So that's what we did. Radhika made damn sure of it.

Terry, Janet, Zach, and Radhika worked together like a well-oiled machine from late April through June. The overlap of wraparound services with the last few months of early intervention services proved to be incredibly valuable. Everyone was on the same page, and I think Teri and Janet also pushed Cam harder those last few weeks at Radhika's very upfront suggestions. Each of them was respectful of the other's craft, and the strides Cam made over those weeks were proof of their incredible team effort.

Cam's third birthday was quickly approaching, which meant graduation from early intervention. When the time came, saying goodbye to Teri and Janet was simply heartbreaking for me. Honestly, I didn't know how to let them go. They helped us to understand Cam and his needs, essentially raising him right alongside us. After spending a year with Cam, they each celebrated their last day with him in their own special way while I silently cried in the corner trying to figure out how to keep them there. It was clear that they knew big things were on the horizon for Cam, and they were both thrilled to have been a part of his journey. Change has always been hard for me to accept, but it truly is the catalyst for growth, and we had to keep moving forward.

Building Puzzles Under Water

Best Laid Plans

At three years old, Cam was set to start pre-school. This was not an easy decision for Justin and me to make. We spent many nights discussing our fears of enrolling him. We had built a small village to help us raise Cam, and now the idea of venturing outside of that bubble was daunting. With Radhika's urging and knowing that Zach would be able to go with him, we made the call. To be honest, I made it at the very last minute, and because of that, there was red tape that needed ironed out before Zach could enter the school. I arranged to be in the classroom with Cam for that first week. The school and the teacher were very accommodating. They understood that Cam may need additional prompting or redirecting, so they assured me that I was welcome, and they would do everything possible to create a supportive environment for Cam.

Getting two kids ready for school in the morning is much different than one, and I admit the first few days felt like I was trying to bottle flies, but thankfully they were both attending the same school. As a matter of fact, Gabby had the same preschool teacher that Cam would have. Because Cam knew the halls of the small school, he marched toward his classroom full of confidence with his light blue backpack in place and the pull straps dragging along the linoleum square tiles.

That week he caught on to the morning routine quickly: hang backpack on his hook, then go to the miniature tables to work on coloring pages while the other kids trickled in. I would stay with him until class started and then take my seat at the teacher's desk piled high with books, which made it easy for me to stay out of sight. He loved the weather bear activity where they would discuss the weather and dress the paper bear with the appropriate paper clothing and accessories. He also loved the morning rooster song and would clap and cheer when the teacher sang it. As for the rest, he couldn't care less about what the class was doing. I found myself balancing on the tiny chairs trying to engage him in the activities at hand. He had his own agenda, and that was to explore the room and play with toys. Who can blame him? For the most part, all his therapies followed his lead.

He was not particularly interested in the other children, which worried me, and during free time he chose to play alone off to the side of the group. But mostly, he was content, and I told myself that things would improve in time. There was, however, one activity that he absolutely hated. When it was time for the bathroom break and dismissal, the teachers would have the kids line up at the door, boys in one line and girls in the other. Somehow, my son, who loved to line up everything within arm's reach, did not like to be lined up himself.

At the time, I didn't understand it and the teachers were just as confused. His reaction was so intense that the teacher asked if I wanted to take him to the bathroom myself. I didn't want to give in, even though he would be in tears. So, instead of removing him from the line, I stood with him and tried to distract him with books from the mini library that was just inside the classroom door.

Up until that point, I had support in waiting out these types of behaviors, but all of a sudden, it wasn't just our circle watching things unfold and offering suggestions.

I was on my own, and for the first time, I had to consider how things would affect others—teachers and his peers alike. I felt a very strange mixture of embarrassment and vulnerability, and it seemed like there was a spotlight on each of us. The kids were also confused: some got upset by it while others tried to console Cam. Would they tell their parents about the little boy who loses his shit in the bathroom line every day? I did, of course, just want to rescue him, and take him to the bathroom myself, but Radhika's influence was too strong. In my mind, I knew that removing him was not the solution, so I offered an alternative to the teacher on the second day, "Maybe put him at the front of the line?" It was the best I could come up with, and my hope was that if he was at the front, he would feel less anxiety. A part of me thought that maybe he was afraid the line would take too long.

Unfortunately, it didn't help, so the next day I asked if they could call each student to the line leaving Cam last, so that he could continue to play until the last second. The teacher explained she did not think she had enough time for that, and she preferred that I just take Cam to the bathroom. Honestly, I was irritated. Yes, I understand she had a schedule to keep but there were only seven students. Cam's reaction was less severe at dismissal time, but on the third day, we were both exhausted and more than ready for the weekend. After he got his backpack on, I took him by the hand, and we headed for the door—no line—fuck it.

I filled Zach in on the week during his time with Cam after school. We consulted with Radhika on the line standing and the lack of peer interaction, and I mentioned the less-than-stellar support given by the teachers. She made plans to go to the school the following week.

Over the next few months, Cam continued to like what he liked and ignored the rest. The TSS (Zach) role within a classroom is to assist when needed; unfortunately Zach was running the show. He was not left with any choice; the teacher and her assistant made no actual attempts to keep Cam engaged. Even with additional prompting and advice from Radhika, they continued to leave Cam out. It was simply a matter of not having the experience or the training, and Justin and I began to worry. Based on Zach's reports back to us, Cam was struggling and was becoming very dependent on him. On the other hand, he was at times modeling his typical peers and even playing with them during free time, as well as taking turns and sharing toys here and there.

Zach mentioned that Cam never spoke to the other children; it was as if he only knew how to speak to adults. There was now a whole new set of concerns. First and foremost, was this even the right environment for Cam? Justin and I agreed that the peer interaction was the most important part, and since Zach was seeing improvement in that area, we would give it some more time. Radhika suggested that during free time, Zach should pull back from Cam to give him a little more independence and space to interact with the other students. Since there was no expectation during free time, we all agreed that this would be the focus. In the meantime, Radhika would continue to try to advise the teacher and her assistant on how to make small concessions and engage Cam in the scheduled activities.

At home, Cam was still making great strides. We were working on two-step directions on everything from taking his shoes off and then placing them in the closet to first cutting out a shape and then pasting it onto another piece of paper. He was doing quite well, better when it was an activity he wanted to do, of course. The team continued to brainstorm ways to get the most out of preschool, but unfortunately, the teacher and her assistant never truly got on board. One morning at pick up, Zach walked Cam out to my car with a look of absolute frustration and anger on his face. The routine was that once I picked up Cam, Zach would meet us at the house for the remainder of the session time. When we got to the house, Zach dropped his bag on the floor and put his hands on his head in complete turmoil.

"You are not going to believe this; I almost don't want to tell you."

Good grief, what was he about to say? My stomach was in knots. I had never seen Zach upset in any way. He proceeded to tell me that during free time, he was sitting at a table close to the teacher's desk writing his notes.

The assistant was teasing the teacher about something, and he went on to say that the assistant started to mime sign language with a muted tone of voice meant to mimic a hearing-impaired person, and said to the teacher, "Are you stupid, do you need help?"

With that, both the teacher and assistant laughed hysterically. I was furious. I called Justin at work immediately. His coworkers heard a slew of explanatory remarks peppered with some very colorful language. How could any teacher (or any adult for that matter) sit in a classroom full of children, not to mention one special needs child, and display such ignorance? I didn't know what to do, but I did know that if I approached the teacher and assistant, I would have needed bail money soon after. I called the principal.

After explaining the issues, we were having and detailing the conversation Zach overheard, the principal said to me, "What would you like me to do?"

There wasn't any concern in her voice. She was irritated with me and did not want to be bothered. The following day, Zach again overheard a conversation between the teacher and the assistant. They were complaining about me. He listened as the teacher called me a coward for calling the principal and not coming to her. *Me? A coward?* All I could do was laugh when he told me, and honestly, I felt very sorry for those women.

As parents, we inherently want our children to be understood and valued, and this is amplified when you have a child with special needs. If you find that someone, no matter their role, is not understanding or valuing your child, cut the loss. Most importantly, understand that it is not *your* loss, it is the other party's loss. Accept that they simply do not have the capacity needed to be a part of the team and move on.

We pulled Cam from the school that day, three months shy of the end of the year. The school made no apologies and no effort to keep Cam as a student. As if that was not bad enough, at the end of the year, we attended the annual school art odyssey as we always did. It was a fun event where each grade had a section in the gym where their artwork for the year was displayed. We were expecting to see both Gabby and Cam's artwork but when we got to the preschool section, all of Cam's peers' artwork was hung but nothing of Cam's was there. We walked down the hall toward the preschool room to inquire about his artwork. The lights were off and the door shut. Just outside the door there was a mess of construction paper rolled up in a rubber band. I noticed that Cam's name was written on the roll, I picked it up and a shower of glitter and dried macaroni hit the floor. It was Cam's artwork for the year. This remains one of the most hurtful moments in my life as a mom of a special needs child. But let's move on.

Justin and I bought our first home just a few months prior to our wedding—a nice little two-story in great condition that sat on a double fenced lot in the city. We were close to everything, and for a young couple it was a great move. We had many firsts in that house; we brought both of our babies home to that house, and held many birthday parties in the backyard, holiday dinners in our tiny dining room, and other various celebrations at the house. It was a very hard decision to make, but it was time for us to move.

The city school district was lacking. Justin had grown up in the city and had a less than positive experience in terms of education. When it was time to enroll Gabby in school, we chose a private school and were mostly happy with the environment. Unfortunately, the experience we had when we enrolled Cam was beyond disappointing, and the eventual gut punch of ignorance forced us to make the decision to research school districts with accredited special education programs.

That summer, we placed our first home together on the market. We chose a district that was on the smaller side, so as not to send Gabby into complete shock—she was used to very small classroom sizes—but also one that was well known for their special needs' programs. We frantically searched for a new home in the school district we had chosen but soon realized we would need to rent versus buy because the price range was out of reach. It was another adjustment that we took on without fear simply because there was no room for it.

"Corn is Awesome"

We found a nice rental house on a great street. It was going to be a stretch in terms of budget, but we were confident it would work out—it had to. We started the lease on the house a month prior to the closing of our house to give us some extra time to get things moved. Over that time, our days consisted of summer outings and therapies. When Justin came home from work, we would move items from the house to the rental. We did not have money to hire a moving company or even a moving truck, so we moved the entire house ourselves, just the two of us in our minivan. It's a wonder we both survived.

Cam's treatment plans became more expansive, covering more ground than I had thought possible. Letters and numbers, shapes, colors, animals, and animal sounds were at the forefront now. Cam was taking it all in: even when you thought he was not listening, he was. He often surprised us with unprompted words, and with that, his little personality was really shining through. He would hold up a flashcard with a car on it and say "dog" with a devilish grin and a wild giggle or label a color wrong with a side eye and raised eyebrow to get a reaction out of us. He loved to make us laugh and was becoming a bit of a ham. We loved every second of it.

Because Cam was able to stay focused for much longer periods of time, we were able to start reading more age-appropriate books with him at bedtime. He would snuggle in, laying his head on our shoulder, and help turn the pages. Sometimes he would try to turn the page mid-sentence with that devilish grin just to make you laugh. He delighted in books that we could read with a repetitive cadence, as you can imagine Dr. Seuss was a huge hit. He took the book, *There Was an Old Lady that Swallowed a Fly* everywhere he went for at least two years. Justin, Gabby, and I knew the book by heart and got really good at reciting it very quickly, which Cam loved. He also loved music, and he loved to dance. If you were in the car and changed the station on a song he was digging, he would let you know, "back, back, back!" He often sang his version of popular songs, and we would sing along with him.

In all, Cam was more engaged with us and with all his helpers coming to the house each day. He was more aware when people entered the room and would often leave what he was doing to greet them. Even with his limited vocabulary, his communication with the outside world was growing with each day. By the end of our first summer with Zach and Radhika, Cam had around 25 to 35 words he used constantly and appropriately, with the exception of his stand-up act of incorrect labels to get a laugh.

Cam and Gabby's relationship was also growing; she loved to play with Cam and teach him new things. Zach had planned a vacation and would not be at the house for a week. We were given the option to have a substitute come in to fulfill Cam's hours, but we decided just to give everyone the week off. By that time, we had almost two years of constant therapy, and a break sounded like a good idea. But Gabby was not sold on it. When that week came,

Monday morning Gabby came downstairs with a bag full of small toys and trinkets, as well as a chart she had made. She let us know that she would be Zach for the week, and she had activities planned that mirrored Zach's.

When Cam would accomplish a task, he was allowed to pick a prize from the bag. She kept notes on her chart to give to Zach when he returned. We let her run with it; I think that maybe she was afraid that, if someone didn't continue the work, Cam might slide backward. That same week, while I was doing dishes, I could hear Gabby and Cam in the next room. Gabby was explaining the game, "Rock, Paper, Scissors." I walked into the room to find her hand over hand teaching Cam the moves. My heart sank a little. I told her that I was not sure Cam was ready for that and he may not be able to play the game just yet. She shrugged me off and continued on. By the end of the day, Cam was playing the game. Anytime Gabby would teach Cam something new, she had a huge advantage over the adults: she never considered the idea that he couldn't achieve something. There was no fear or worry for her, just a big sister teaching her little brother a new game. When Zach came back the following week, Gabby presented her progress chart. Zach was blown away.

I said, "She also taught him how to play 'Rock, Paper, Scissors.'"

Zach's reply, "Of course she did." Gabby was eight years old.

Amid all the summer fun and goals being achieved, we started seeing, or I guess you could say "hearing," more vocal stims from Cam. He could get very caught up in them, and at times, they would interfere with his learning and time on task. It was very frustrating. When he would really get going, it was as if he could not hear us at all, and at times, we simply had to wait it out. We were still providing Cam with a sensory diet twice a day, but as he got older, and more and more was expected of him, I believe he used the vocal stims to stay focused or possibly to drown us out when he felt overwhelmed.

Dr. T. once told me that he thinks parents, and often therapists, are too quick to want to get rid of self-stimulatory behaviors, but the reality is, these kids need them. Yes, we can provide a sensory diet, but that doesn't mean if the need for the input strikes, they won't provide it for themselves in some way.

He said, "If it is not interfering with learning or communicating at the time he is doing it, let him do it."

I remembered Janet from early intervention told me that verbal and vocal stims could be harder to redirect than others. These types of stims provide immediate input, but there are some other activities that can help, like blowing up balloons or using a straw to blow a cotton ball across a table. Whistles work well and even hard crunchy snacks. When Cam would become sidetracked by verbal stims during therapy, we would use these tools to get him on track, and it usually helped. The times that it didn't, I understood that, for whatever reason, he needed those stims and would let him do his thing. Sometimes I would join in; I have to say it is fun.

As we got closer to the closing of our house, we decided to have one last cookout. I invited my sister over and then got to work cleaning up the patio and getting out the push bikes and the sprinkler. When Maura arrived, we hit the backyard to enjoy the sunshine. Justin grilled burgers, while Gab and Maura shucked corn. Cam and I both took several runs down the yard on his push bikes.

Ever since Zach showed Cam the thrill of speed, he was never happy with pushing around the flat part of the yard again. We would start halfway up the hill, but Cam would always try to start at the top. Eventually, we made our way inside to have dinner. Content with our fine day, no one was thinking about stims or therapy or autism, for that matter.

As we sat chatting and enjoying our meal, Cam was feverishly devouring an ear of corn, and out of nowhere, a few weeks shy of his fourth birthday, Cam quietly spoke his first full sentence. We jumped up in astonishment, all of us were clapping, cheering, and laughing through tears. Cam looked around at us with wide eyes and started kicking his legs under the table. With a giant kernel-laden smile and butter dripping down his chin, he said it again, loud and proud, "Corn is awesome!"

Building Puzzles Under Water

Shit Happens

As important as it is to detail Cam's successes, I think it is equally important to detail the tough times too. Cam's therapies surely brought about frustration for him, and in turn, the rest of us. He could shut down without warning ... and still does. If you talk *at* Cam too much, he will disengage without so much as an *I need a break*. And some days, once you lost him, that was it for the day. Better luck tomorrow. Cam continued wanting to fold tea towels perfectly and other activities that, if it didn't go exactly to plan, he would become completely inconsolable. Often, it was very hard to redirect him. He would cry so intensely that he would end up choking and sometimes even vomit.

New stims would pop up out of the blue, and some became obstacles for him. There was a time when he would hold one hand in a tight first for hours at a time, it seemed. I'm talking white knuckles and fingernail marks in his palm when he would finally release it. We tried everything to get him to stop. I would give him a toy to hold in his other hand and then a favorite snack with the hopes that he would let go of the fist, but instead, he would just put down the toy to use his free hand to take the snack. I bought a drum and drumsticks hoping that would be tempting enough to make him let go, but Cam would just bang on the drum with one hand. I tried anything that would require two hands, but not even his beloved tinker toys were desirable enough. This went on for weeks and was very hard to watch.

At the time, Gabby had packs and packs of what looked like seeds that would *grow* in water and turned to little colorful gelatinous beads overnight. I thought just maybe this would do the trick, so I grew a bowl of them one night and presented them to Cam the next time he was stuck in the stim. As the universe would have it, it worked. I took both of his hands and plunged them into the bowl, the beads were cold to the touch and squishy. At first Cam seemed to be wondering what the hell this was, but then I felt his fist open under my grasp and he began to mix them around with both hands. For several weeks we kept a bowl of these beads at the ready so anytime he would hold his fist for more than a few minutes, we would give him the bowl. Eventually, the stim faded away, and we never saw that particular stim again. This is not an uncommon theme, and Cam has had many "one-off stims," as we call them. Something new would pop up for a few weeks, just long enough to make us worry, and then disappear without a trace.

Even though we saw quick progress in many areas, some things took a bit more time and patience. There was one particular goal that took years, four to be exact. When Cam was two years old, we started potty training. There was no therapy involved here, just two parents starting the potty-training process when the books say you should. We bought him the little potty and started sitting him on it with pages to color or small toys to play with. We had a book of small stickers that were only used for the potty, and when Cam was successful, we would try to have him put a sticker in a little notebook. He preferred to stick them right to the outside of the potty bowl; in the interest of choosing our battles, we went with it. He caught on to peeing in the potty fairly quickly, and we were pleasantly surprised. We did all the potty celebrations: clapping, cheering, rewards, and stickers just like any other parents would do. Justin even composed a freestyle rap about peeing in the potty, which Cam loved. Cam would stand and clap and sometimes point at his success. Before long, he graduated to training pants. We were on track, easy peasy.

The other end of potty training was not coming about so easily. The dreaded number two. Cam had a very regimented pooping schedule: every night between 7 p.m. and 8 p.m., like clockwork. We would sit him on the potty, but he would immediately get up and try to get his training pants back on. He would get very upset and seemed to be scared of the process. He never did this during the day and was using the potty on his own to pee regularly. We decided to give him a bit more time and let him continue to use his training pants in the evening. The bottom line is we were less diligent because we were exhausted from the day. The evening bath and bedtime routines for the children made us almost giddy; it's the time of the day when parents know that soon the house will be quiet. So yeah, we let it slide.

It wasn't until Radhika arrived on the scene and started asking questions that we started to feel pressure to get it done. She would check up on all his self-help abilities— things like using utensils, early stages of dressing himself, and yes, potty training. These were not things that were involved in his therapy with Zach, but Radhika left no stone unturned when it came to Cam. He was quite adept at most things involving self-help, but he was still taking a poo in his training pants every night at 8 p.m., while standing in front of the TV. At one point, when Cam was around four years old, yes four, Radhika suggested making Cam clean up after himself. She said to still take the training pants off for him and clean him up but make him roll up the pants, put them in the bag, and throw them away. It was worth a try. I thought for sure Cam would hate it, and maybe, just maybe, he would see the light, but his attitude toward it was like, *yeah, no problem, see you tomorrow at 8* and took care of the trash like it was nothing. Then she said to at least make him stand in the bathroom, not in front of the TV. She was getting frustrated with us. In hindsight, I get it, but at the time, it irritated me. Still, I had to admit it made sense. At the very least, he should be in the appropriate room.

By this time, several more months had gone by, and Cam was well attached to his routine. He hated it. He wanted to watch his show and poop in peace. We did persist, and after some time, Cam would eventually get a pair of training pants out of the package and head to the bathroom on his own. He was never happy about it, but he did it. During an appointment with Dr T., Radhika brought it up. (*Dammit Radhika, shhhh!*) By the way, once she was on the team, she came to all of Cam's appointments, which I loved ... until that day. But as always, Dr. T. was understanding and said after a bit of contemplation with his hand to his chin, "It may be a sensory thing for him. The pressure of the pants themselves, there is security there."

He suggested having Cam sit on the toilet with the training pants on until he got comfortable sitting there and then stop with the training pants. That night, we bought one of those mini toilet seat inserts with cartoon characters in the hopes to entice him a bit. When 8 p.m. rolled around, we put Cam on the seat in his training pants. He looked at me like I had lost my damn mind and immediately jumped off and ran. The next night I augmented the plan and tried to have him stand on the toilet seat, seat down of course—I'm not that crazy. Cam was so confused, but he did like climbing on things, so it worked. This continued for months. During the day, I would randomly have him sit on the potty—just to sit—lid down with a toy or a book in the hopes he would become more comfortable sitting there.

Then one night, we tried to have him sit on the potty again with the pants on, and he did not jump off. He was finally comfortable sitting and pooping. What a weird thing to say. The first time we tried to get him to sit without the pants he screamed and cried, he was *not* ready for that step, but by this time, he was five. I hate to say it, but we grew tired of wheeling and dealing with the kid, so one night, without him knowing, I cut a hole in those damn training pants. Justin kept his attention while I slipped them on him, and he sat without noticing the hole. I had never been more nervous to get caught in something in my entire life. I sat on the floor and waited, as usual. The flight risk was always there so it was a necessary evil. Then it happened, *plop*, he looked up at me with wide eyes.

He looked scared and confused, "What was that?"

I said, "That was your poop going in the potty where it belongs."

He was really mad at me. There was no celebration from him even though I was hooting and hollering. For the next few weeks, he checked to make sure there was no hole. Eventually I tried it again, only this time with warning and coaxing, and Cam eventually gave in. Justin and I took turns cutting holes in training pants for months on end. We would try to get him to sit without them here and there, but he just could not do it without what seemed like absolute fear.

Over time, we would make the hole larger and larger. We eventually transitioned to cutting holes in underwear and ditched the training pants all together. Cam did not seem to mind that, as long as something was around his waist. Looking back, the process was unreal, but there was no other way for him. We got to the point where all that was left of the underwear was the waistband; we called it the "poop belt." So, 8 p.m. would roll around, and the regular underwear came off and the poop belt went on. This went on for close to a full year. Sometimes you just have to honor the stages of progress. Even Radhika settled into the idea of the poop belt and Dr. T. commended us on our ingenuity.

One afternoon the four of us were watching a movie, likely for the third or fourth time that day, as Cam loves to rewatch his favorite films over and over and back-to-back.

It was not even close to the golden hour when Cam popped up from the couch and said, "I have to poop!"

He ran down the hall to the bathroom, and the rest of us froze. Cam hit the bathroom and went about his business. Justin, Gabby, and I were silent as we started to look down the hall then back at each other over and over like it was Wimbledon, circa 1979.

He finished, washed up, and ran back into the living room saying, "Play it again, play it again!" pointing to the TV.

And just like that, at six years old, Cam retired the poop belt on his own. You may be wondering how we got away with this when it came to starting school on time. Well, we lied. Cam's schedule was so reliable up until that day that we simply were not worried. Admittedly, it was not a responsible move, and I do not recommend playing this risky game. If you have a special needs child that is not fully potty trained in time for preschool, please have an open conversation with the program or school you are considering. More than likely, you will be able to make accommodations.

Building Puzzles Under Water

IEPs and 123s

We moved into the rental house with a little over a month left of summer. By that time, I had found out about a preschool program in the area called DART, which stands for "discovery, assessment, referral, and tracking." The program provides free screening and evaluations to identify needs in everything from communication to cognitive abilities. The classrooms included both special needs children and typical children and are run by teachers with special education backgrounds. I had Cam evaluated and registered before the last box was moved to the new house—everything was falling into place. The evaluation was very similar to all the ones that came before it, and Cam was approved for the five-day-a-week program.

The kids did well with the move. Cam was excited to explore the new house and yard, which was much larger than our old yard. It had two levels that were perfect for running and climbing, and at the top of the yard, there was a swing ... Cam's favorite. The neighborhood was full of kids, and although Gabby was a bit nervous at first, she was a part of the gang riding bikes up and down the street in no time.

The new school year began, and Cam's school was 15 minutes away from Gabby's school which gave me just enough time to drop him off and then get her to school with only minutes to spare. Cam handled drop off much better than Gabby and I did. On that first day, the two of us had teary eyes. It was hard for both of us to watch him walk off without one of us or one of his team members. Cam was a little apprehensive those first few days, but the teachers were great. They met the kids in the vestibule of the school instead of having the parents walk them to the classroom, which I think made it an easier transition for all of us. Gabby and I would say our goodbyes to Cam and then rush to the car to get her to school.

The first week, Cam's daily notes were positive—he followed directions, focused, and worked hard. Cam had learned to do these things over the previous two years. The daily notes are both a blessing and a curse. On good days, they provide relief, and on bad days stress. At this point, I have read approximately 1,320 daily notes. Somewhere around 800, I learned to only stress about the not-so-great days if I was seeing a pattern of behaviors.

One of the scores on the daily notes was peer interaction, and Cam generally scored low in this area. Rather content in class, he was very solitary, despite the teacher's efforts to guide him in interactions. On the other hand, he was a Chatty Cathy with the adults in the room. It was something to work on. By winter, Cam was displaying great confidence inside and outside of the classroom. When we would get home from school, we would have him show us his work and his daily notes in an effort to assign some responsibility to him outside of school.

His time with Zach would be filled with follow-through from the things he worked on in class, his focus better than ever. He was able to play simple board games with us but seemed to still play with toys inappropriately. Lining up or stacking toys was still a favorite. He also liked wrapping them up in towels or pushing them between the couch cushions.

I realized that he simply did not have pretend play skills, even though we would often play with his playsets together. We would create stories and naturally play pretend, but Cam did not do it. It became a mission to teach Cam how to play make believe. We spent countless hours—all of us, even Gabby—playing with his play sets. We created elaborate stories of his favorite figurines going on camping trips, or going to the park, the zoo, and so on. Often using a hand-over-hand technique to show Cam how to move the figures from one spot to the next. He enjoyed the stories, but it took several months for him to join in. Eventually, he did.

On the flip side, he did have a great imagination when it came to his love of building. At this point the LEGOs, blocks, and Tinker Toys no longer seemed enough for Cam, and he started to build what I would call "simple machines" out of household items. His builds would always have a working mechanism or two. One of my favorites was one he made that same year. We had just put up the Christmas tree, and I headed to the kitchen to start dinner.

Cam came in and said, "need little cup" and pointed at the kitchen cabinets.

I thought he meant one of his small plastic cups, so I handed him one.

"No, little cup, little cup," he was not happy I gave him the wrong cup and pointed to a cabinet that did not even have cups!

I told him that was the smallest cup we had, but he persisted, "little cup, little cup!"

I finally opened the cabinet he was pointing at, which is where we kept our medicine bin. I realized he wanted one of the medicine cups.

"This Cam?"

He jumped up and down shouting, "Yes, yes, yes!"

I gave it to him, and off he went. He came in a few minutes later and helped himself to a roll of tape from our kitchen junk drawer. About 15 minutes later, I heard Gabby say, "Whoa Cam, that is awesome."

I headed into the living room. Cam had been playing with a helium balloon all day, something Justin would often pick up for Cam as a prize for good days at school. It was a bit of a running joke: the guy in a minivan buying a single helium balloon at the grocery store. So, I walked into the living room to find that Cam had tied the end of the balloon ribbon to a leg of the TV stand. He stretched the ribbon across the living room and placed a large empty spool that held our Christmas lights on the balloon to hold it down to the floor. Then he took a small piece of yarn, taped it on either side of the cup around the balloon ribbon, making a basket of sorts, and inside the cup was a little green army guy. Cam removed the spool releasing the helium balloon, and as it rose, the little cup slid down the ribbon making it to the bottom of the string. The kid was four and he made stuff like this all the time ... and he still does.

Cam's four-year-old preschool experience was far different from year three. He was in a supportive and understanding environment and, in all, thrived. He applied the skills he learned in and out of the classroom and continued to display confidence and growth throughout the year. It was a great fit. Gabby also did very well her first year in the new school. I remember how quickly the kids started to call her "Gibs." She was like Norm from *Cheers*. She would walk into school, and you would hear "Gibs!" from several corners of the hall. Life was good. By the end of that summer, Cam was on track to attend kindergarten.

The school district that we moved to had a kindergarten program with a coteaching model. Within the typical classroom, there is a teacher, a special education teacher who monitors and steps in when support is needed, and a paraprofessional (para) assigned to each student. Cam would be with typical peers and special needs peers all learning the same curriculum.

The school was also equipped with a sensory room, which was essential for Cam. In my opinion, all schools should have a sensory room. These rooms are dedicated to sensory input: including trampolines and pedal bikes, bins of sand or beans with funnels, and mini shovels, swings, brushes for skin brushing, hula hoops, putty, and play dough. Truly, the sky should be the limit, when designing a place for kids with sensory needs to take a break and be free to work through those needs throughout the day in a safe and understanding environment. It is invaluable.

We were so excited about Cam entering kindergarten on time and with skills we were told he would never have. This accomplishment was not lost on us. Justin and I would sometimes just look at each other in the midst of all the change, therapies, and people in and out of our house and take a deep breath—smiles on our faces—we were killing it.

All the necessary paperwork was complete for kindergarten, and we were scheduled to attend the teddy bear picnic just before the start of school. The picnic is to welcome the incoming kindergartners, and the kids bring their favorite teddy bear. I assume the teddy bears are to help the kids feel more at ease. In Cam's case, a "ho" picnic would have been better since he was not much into teddy bears and still took his pillow everywhere he went. But we would make it work by taking a special trip to the store for Cam to pick out a teddy bear.

Just before the picnic, we received a call from the director of special education who gave us the contact information for the school psychologist. We were to make an appointment with her so she could evaluate Cam and construct his very first individualized education program (IEP). This uses the needs of the individual child to adjust the curriculum, if needed. This is also a means to make additions to the school day such as speech therapies, sensory room breaks, and extra time needed on tasks. The list could be endless as it is truly individualized. We arrived at the school for our appointment with Cam wearing a necklace he recently made from his tinker toys. He insisted on wearing it. I was a bit concerned he would be distracted by it, but I let him wear it. After all, accessories are a must to complete any outfit. The psychologist greeted us in the lobby of the school. She introduced herself to me, shook my hand, and then bent down to meet Cam on his level.

She immediately said, "Oh Cam, I love your necklace."

To which my son corrected her and said, "It's an amulet."

I burst into laughter. She looked at me and said "Wow, that's a word!" and began to laugh too.

Cam was irritated, *What the hell was so funny?* It was clearly an amulet, so he repeated himself in a tone that resembled Radhika's get-your-shit-together tone. Brilliant.

After the evaluation, the psychologist told me that she would write the IEP and send us the preliminary copy, and a meeting would be scheduled—the ominous IEP meeting. By this time, I was following several autism-related social media pages, as well as blogs and other outlets. I had heard and read so many disheartening stories about IEP meetings, heated arguments, parents not being heard, and programs not being followed, so I was a bit on edge. Justin and I would attend and, not surprisingly, Radhika asked if she could come along.

We entered the room to find the principal, both teachers, the speech therapist, and the director of special education in attendance. Not at all intimidating. The three of us took our seats. Prior to the event, we had poured over the draft, so we were ready for the meeting. New to us, Justin and I felt as though all the boxes were checked, but Radhika noticed that there was nothing listed to allow for sensory breaks or extended time on assessments. So, we made notes in the margins of the draft. By accident, we established our IEP M.O., or modus operandi. We sat and listened to the *powers that be* go over the draft, and then when they were finished, we referred to our marked-up draft with the additions we wanted. We were able to confidently tell, not ask, the team for sensory breaks and extended times to be added.

I have to give credit to Radhika on this one. I learned from her that you don't ask: you arm yourself with knowledge, and you come prepared and request with confidence. I have approached every IEP meeting since with the same style and have never, not once, been denied a request. We get the draft, Justin and I set aside time to go over it together with a fine-toothed comb and our trusty red pen. We mark the margin with any questions, if we want things to be added we make notes in the appropriate section, and then we put it neatly back in the envelope it came in.

On meeting day, we let everyone read their sections, in our case it's usually the teacher, the special education teacher, and the speech therapist. The principal and director of special education oversee the meetings. We listen and nod, and then when they are done, as they pass out copies to be signed, we pull ours out and make our requests. Typically, we have the updated copy within the week. No one wants a battle, and if they do, it's very hard to battle someone who has their shit together. My best advice here is not to go into IEP meetings ready for a fight, but go into them prepared and knowing without a doubt, that you will leave with what you want.

In the time between the IEP meeting and the kindergarten welcome picnic, Cam had his second graduation from therapies. I had been taking him to on-site speech and occupational therapies for almost a year. His skill level was such that he would be released from these therapies with the knowledge that he would have continued support in school.

On that last day, as we walked out of the facility I said, "Can you believe it Cam? You are all done!"

I got him buckled into the car, and he reached up and offered me a high five. "We did it!" he shouted.

Yes, we did kiddo. I started to tear up and suggested we get a cake to celebrate. My little man replied, "I prefer doughnuts."

My five-year-old used the word "prefer." I couldn't help but giggle. We stopped for doughnuts on the way home, and that afternoon once Justin was home from work the four of us proceeded to eat the entire dozen.

The morning of the teddy bear picnic, we were all set. Cam had his new teddy bear and brown bag lunch ready to go. The picnic was held in the school yard, which had a really nice playground with miniature climbing rocks, some with slides, little swings, and teeter totters all brightly colored and perfectly cheerful. There were picnic tables set up with chips and cookies and others with arts and crafts with a teddy bear theme. We had a chance to talk with the kindergarten teacher and the special education teacher in a far less intimidating environment from the IEP meeting. They were extremely welcoming and kind.

Justin and I did our best to make the awkward small talk with the other parents, but we both had an eye on Cam. He was not engaging with the other kids. He moved from swings to slides and back again. He did take turns, which was nice to see, but some of the kids asked him name, and he just walked away. It was a little heartbreaking to watch a gaggle of typical kids do their typical things while Cam remained silent other than the occasional verbal stim. As the picnic came to an end, the teacher announced to the kids that it was time for the bus ride. Excuse me, what? How did we miss this on the agenda? The kids would be getting on a school bus and taking about a twenty-minute ride around the neighborhood while the parents stayed back. I looked at Justin terrified. My entire body was full of knots.

"He can't do that." I whispered to Justin. There was no doubt in my mind we would be skipping the neighborhood tour.

He took my hand and said, "We have to let him try. I am sure they will assign him an adult to sit with."

I wanted to throat punch him—no way. But I knew he was right, so instead of physical violence, I made a beeline for the teacher while the parents were telling their kids to behave and making sure they had their teddy bears.

I asked if someone would be with Cam, "Oh yes, of course. We have a few teachers and paras that will be sitting with the kids with special needs."

OK fine, but still, I wanted to grab him and run. We watched Cam climb the stairs of the bus. He was excited and showed no sign of nervousness. After he disappeared up the stairs, the next 20 minutes were lost. I do not remember anything, not a single conversation with Justin, or other parents for that matter. I only remember fear. The bus returned, and I don't how long after—maybe two to three weeks—I was able to breathe again. Cam bounced off with one of the paraprofessionals and ran toward us, threw the bear in our direction, and headed straight for the swings.

OK then.

The para said he did great and that he was a sweet little boy. She said she could tell right away that he would do great. I spent the rest of the day feeling snubbed, how could he leave me so easily and be sweet to another woman, for that matter? Of course, I'm kidding, well ... half kidding.

For me to detail the next several school years I would have to write a series of books—maybe someday—but for now, I will detail some of the key highs and lows. Cam was doing very well in kindergarten; he was able to remain on task for the most part. We could tell from his daily notes that when it seemed he needed a break his para would take him to the sensory room. He won over the hearts of all his teachers. I remember one day one of the teachers came out at dismissal beaming and told me that Cam had complimented her boots in the middle of class. She also told me that the speech therapist was smitten with Cam and would oftentimes let him cuddle up to her, which I was told was not her normal way of doing things.

His daily notes were mostly very positive with the occasional meltdown of either crying fits or angry protests to certain assignments. Generally, it was the longer, slower projects that he seemed to get overwhelmed by. We worked on these things in therapy with Zach when he would meet us at the house in the afternoon. Radhika had offered a very simple solution to the lengthier workbook pages that seemed to set Cam off. She spoke with the teachers at her next school visit and suggested that they simply cover half of the page. She also suggested offering just the odd or even numbers if it was clear that Cam was understanding the lessons.

Toward the end of the year, we seemed to get more and more notes about Cam having crying fits. We were also seeing it more at home as well. It was confusing. By the time he started kindergarten, he was able to stay focused and on task for 20 to 30 minutes, but now, things seemed to be going backward. We were all genuinely concerned that what we were seeing was regression. The mystery was solved at his IEP meeting for first grade.

Usually held in the month of April, we found out just a few months shy of the end of his kindergarten year that the special education teacher was allowing Cam to stop working when he got upset, often giving him a tablet to play with or taking him to the sensory room. The teachers went on to tell me that one of the other students on the spectrum had a very disruptive reaction anytime any of the kids became upset. To my recollection, her reactions were quite intense, and she would often dart out of the room and down the hallway. So, the solution was to keep Cam as calm as possible.

My kid was not regressing; he learned that if he made a big enough stink, he wouldn't have to do the work. I was in total disbelief; I could not understand why they did not come to me with more detailed information on how Cam was handling things at school. A short note that says, "Cam became upset today during reading," is far different from "We are constantly removing Cam from class," or "Cam was not required to do his work because he was crying." I was a bit stunned, but thankfully, Radhika was there and offered some additional solutions. When we left, she was just as angry at the situation as I was.

That night, after going over everything with Justin, we decided to request that Cam not be placed in the same classroom with this student the following year. I called the director of special education and explained what had been happening in the classroom for months and that we felt it was not in the best interest for both children to be in the same classroom again. It was a very hard call to make as Cam and the other child had become friends.

They knew each other from the waiting room at on-site speech and occupational therapy. His friend also attended the program we placed Cam in after the pre-school debacle. I had become friends with this child's mother. They had play dates often, and she and I would get together during school hours to sit and chat. Unfortunately, she did not take the news well. She seemed to somehow be offended and ended our friendship. That was very hard for me.

The hits didn't stop there; toward the end of the school year, Zach came to me with news. He would be moving forward on his career path and taking a position above the TSS level. I was crushed. He had been with us for so long that he knew Cam the way we knew Cam; he was one of us. Losing him at such a crucial time was almost more than I could handle. I cannot detail his last day with us because I honestly think it is wiped from my memory. When I reached out to Zach to ask his permission to use his name in this book, it had been several years since we talked. His response floored me, so I will share it to display what a wonderful and kind person he is.

Zach responded, "It would be my honor. I don't think I can fully express to you and Cam how thankful I am for you guys. You have impacted my life at a level that has not only changed me as a clinician but, more importantly, how your family and your son have shaped me into the person I am today."

If you ask Cam today about Zach, he still remembers him. They were great friends, and that friendship helped to shape Cam into the young man he is today.

Radhika hand-picked Zach's replacement. She assured me that Nicole had much to bring to the table. Incredibly sweet and patient, Nicole moved in with ease. She had a beautiful smile that warmed the room and a very calming nature, but she meant business when it was time to work. Cam liked her. He would display the same time-on-task measurements that he did with Zach. He continued to joke around one minute then be sweet as pie the next. He would throw a fit or two during the week, but Nicole always took it in stride.

At the time, Cam had been carrying around a wand that he made from his Tinker Toys, and one afternoon while Nicole was reading to him, he was disinterested, so he waved his wand at her and said, "Abracadabra, disappear!" I immediately told Cam that was not nice, but Nicole thought it was hilarious. She was not offended by it in the least and used the situation to instill in Cam that if he needed a break all he had to do was ask. She told him, "Cam, if you need a break say, 'Miss Nicole, may I have a break?'" He followed her direction, and she granted his wish and set a timer.

When it was time to come back Cam had composed himself and finished the afternoon with focused attention.

Nicole continued the prescribed hours through the end of the school year and through the summer. Radhika was right, as usual. Nicole was a great fit, and I believed she truly helped Cam learn self-advocacy, which led him to gain more self-confidence. Although her time with us was short in comparison to Zach's time with us, she made a huge impact, for which I am incredibly grateful. The additional skills Cam learned over that summer led Radhika to believe that, once he started first grade, it would be time for Cam to graduate from TSS services. Holy cow, what! She was confident that Cam was going to continue to grow with the services at school. She would stay on his case to continue visits in the school, but as far as TSS hours, those were no longer needed. Radhika would be our eyes and ears, our on-site advocate and super sleuth, inside the halls of that school for the next two years.

The changes didn't end there though, with Cam heading into full day school, I was able to go back to work. It was a bit hard for me, as I had been so consumed with being a mom of a special needs child that leaving that hat at home and going back to work was a strange transition. At times, I wished Radhika would visit and create an individualized plan for me, but soon I was back in the swing of things. It was like riding a bike, as they say, and by the following year, Justin and I were able to purchase a home and leave the rental house behind.

The co-teaching program in the school district was offered in kindergarten only. Cam's IEP for first grade had him in the special education classroom for math, reading, and language arts with the first and second grade special education teacher. For all the other classes, he was in the typical classroom with a paraprofessional. Cam's new special education teacher was a force. She was perfect for Cam; she got him. She knew that Cam was always paying attention even when it seemed he was in the clouds. She knew exactly how much pressure to put on him and when to back off a bit. She never removed work from Cam to calm his outburst but, rather, gave him choices of when and how to complete his work. He responded to it very well, and by the end of the day, he would have all his work completed.

Radhika was one of her biggest fans, which is saying a lot. Radhika's expectations are high, for everyone, and Cam's teacher met them with flying colors. In fact, when it was time for Cam's third-grade IEP meeting, Radhika approached me and said that we needed to try to keep Cam with his current teacher. He was soaring academically, and she was not a fan of him moving to a new teacher. Justin and I agreed. She had been so impactful and was very communicative with us, constantly keeping us in the loop with any and all augmentations to the curriculum and patterns of behavior so we could work on things at home. She was a true champion for Cam's growth.

The bad news is that the school was not able to accommodate our request to keep Cam in her classroom. Her schedule with the incoming first and second graders simply could not be adjusted. Radhika and I did everything we could to make it clear during the third grade IEP meeting that Cam's new special education teacher needed to understand how to handle Cam and keep him on track.

She would need to constantly raise the bar by recognizing and utilizing Cam's strengths while making accommodations that fostered growth based on his weaknesses.

We all knew of this new teacher, and to be frank, she was very over the top. She didn't seem very genuine, and anytime she approached Cam in the hallways, he would back away. She was too much for him, like a sensory overload in human form. Cam would have this teacher through fourth grade, and we were a bit worried. The good news is that Cam would be in the third-grade special education classroom for reading and language arts only. As for his math skills, they were on par with his typical classmates, so he was placed in the typical classroom. What an accomplishment so early on! Justin and I were beyond proud.

Unfortunately, the next two years were a bit of a nightmare. Academically, Cam was doing well in his typical classes. Many of his teachers would reach out to us and compliment his drive to work hard, but with reading and language arts, not so much. From the start, Cam displayed anxiety when it came to these subjects. He can get preoccupied with how long things will take, and the longer, the more stressed he gets. Pages full of paragraphs to read or blank lines to fill in make him very nervous. At home, when we would work on practice sheets, we would just cover half the page so that, visually, it was less overwhelming to him. We have always highlighted this anxiety and preoccupation in his IEP meetings, even to this day.

I don't honestly know where this came from, but it is something we continuously work on. I do know that, because of this, he is not a fan of reading or writing and hates to write more than a sentence or two. His comprehension has always been great, but his reading fluency has always been lacking. These were also subjects discussed in every IEP meeting.

Over time, it became clear that his anxiety over lengthy assignments was affecting his ability to excel in these two subjects. Every day for the first few months of third grade, Cam would bring home a mess of papers requiring him to write his address, phone number, my name and Justin's, our cell phone numbers, and other information over and over. In conjunction, we were getting more and more notes sent home about Cam becoming very upset and inconsolable in these classes. We were constantly asking for additional information surrounding these behaviors.

One afternoon, Radhika and I were discussing the notes, and I mentioned to her that the amount of busy work coming home in his folder was excessive. She suggested we approach the teacher and ask her to find other things for Cam to work on. She felt as though he was likely bored, and the monotony of the busywork was frustrating for him. At that point, he could rattle off his address in his sleep. Unfortunately, his teacher did not agree with us and continued to give the assignments to him. There were other suggestions Radhika gave her that she simply would not do. It seemed as though nothing was individualized that year.

Partway through third grade Cam started to become very upset every Friday morning. Weird. Through tears, he would say he didn't want to go to school, that he hated school and begged not to go. We had never seen anything like this from Cam. After a few weeks of this, Cam finally told us why he hated Fridays so much. A few weeks prior, on a Friday, Cam had not finished his work in the special education classroom, so his teacher pulled him from recess after lunch to finish his work in her room. He also told us that, a few times, he was late for social studies because she would keep him back to finish work.

What in the actual hell was she thinking?

Cam's anxiety over how long things take was now off the charts. Justin and I were livid. When I told Radhika about it, I thought she was going to implode with anger. I wrote the teacher an email asking that she call me. Instead, she replied to the email asking what I needed to speak to her about. She would not call me, so I detailed the hell we had been going through for the last several Fridays and to not, under any circumstances, keep Cam from recess or arriving at his other classes on time again. This was honestly the tip of the iceberg. We ran into many similar situations, and, unfortunately, the teacher never got on board. Anytime Radhika or I approached her with ideas on how to individualize Cam's education or ways to minimize behavior brought on by anxiety, we were met with opposition. Every visit Radhika had in the school setting was focused on those two classes for the rest of the year. By the time his IEP for fourth grade rolled around, Cam, Justin, Radhika, and I were exhausted.

The district hired a second director of special education to split the grades between them. Dr. Q. was now the go-to for students in kindergarten through sixth grade. The announcement was made shortly before Cam's fourth-grade IEP. I decided to make an appointment with her so I could discuss Cam's achievements, needs, and the unfortunate shit-show that third grade had become. When I met with her, she had a very firm handshake for such a tiny woman. She has a calm demeanor yet a commanding personality. When she talks, you better listen because she is not going to repeat herself. I loved her immediately. We sat down and got straight to it. My first order of business was to give Dr. Q. a clear understanding of how hard my son, our family, and Cam's helpers have worked to get him to where he was at that time. I explained to her that we were told he would never speak, much less make it to third grade in a typical school setting. I started to tell her about the ways in which we worked to bring about speech.

When I started to talk about the swing in the middle of my living room, her hands went up in the air then crashed down to the table and her eyes were as big as saucers, "Oh my God, I know your family. I know Cam! I know about the swing! Zach! Zach worked with Cam!"

Holy shit. I didn't know what to say, and I distinctly remember feeling a complete sense of relief and hope. Dr. Q. went on to tell me that she had worked with Zach for a few years and that he told Cam's story often. Of course, he didn't use names, but when I brought up the swing, she knew it was us. After talking a bit about how wonderful Zach is, I detailed the issues we had throughout the year, backed up by email threads between the teacher and me that would make your head spin. One of our biggest concerns was that we would not find out about patterns of behavior for weeks and even months at a time. Once I was finished, she said, "Well, this is not good." IEP day came, and Dr. Q. arrived on the scene with great recommendations to make Cam's fourth-grade year run more smoothly. She made it very clear that the recommendations were not suggestions, they were to be followed. Radhika was very hopeful and impressed with Dr. Q.

I found out a few months into summer exactly why she seemed so relieved after meeting Dr. Q. Cam no longer showed enough deficiency to warrant wraparound services. We would enter fourth grade without Radhika.

Fourth grade was a bit less of a nightmare, but to be honest, Justin and I had a secret countdown to the last day of the school year to keep our sanity. We did receive better communication throughout the beginning of the year. At Radhika's suggestion, we had requested at Cam's last IEP that a separate take-home folder be created. Any work that he did not complete in class would go into that folder for Justin and me to help him complete at home. It was a simple yet brilliant idea that helped Cam trust he would not be held back from recess or from making it to his next class on time.

Cam continued to display anxiety in school, and there were still plenty of meltdowns. Communication from his teacher started to drop off, and we were back to receiving ambiguous notes saying things like "Cam was teary today." We noticed him shutting down more often, and he rarely could detail the events that caused such notes to come home. Again, we were in the dark.

I called Radhika, and together we were able to get new BSC hours approved. It was a tough call to make because we had celebrated his success with wraparound services and managed to feel confident without them. In some ways, it felt like we failed Cam, but asking for help does not mean failure. Radhika was back and doing her best to get through to the teacher.

Toward the end of the year, I had an email detailing an issue Cam had in reading class. He had gotten upset and was completely beside himself crying and screaming and had to be removed from class. In the email the teacher wrote that she was "confounded" by Cam's behavior. I was in complete disbelief; Radhika and I spent nearly two years trying to help her understand his anxiety and give her solutions that worked at home and in other classes for Cam.

She also mentioned in one of her emails that she often asked Cam, "Is this how fourth graders act?" or "Is this a big problem or a little problem?" We were so close to the end of the year, and I was so tired from the battle that I almost did not respond. But I kept wondering how she thought saying those things to Cam, or any child for that matter, was helpful. I gave myself some time to calm down before responding. In my email, I thanked her for the information and asked that she not speak to my son in that way. I explained that the only thing she achieved by asking Cam those questions was to add shame and guilt to his anxiety and that he was left to work through those emotions without any understanding or assistance from an adult. I went on to say that when he is upset—no matter the reason—it is a big problem to him. That was my last correspondence with her until Cam's IEP meeting for fifth grade. Thankfully, the end was near.

To our complete delight, fifth and sixth grade middle school was what dreams are made of. A night to day transformation in all things special education related. Cam's new teacher was everything we could hope for. Patient, calming, open and intuitive are just a few words to describe her style of teaching. Cam was with her for reading and language arts. She understood his anxiety related to these subjects and was able to work with him one-on-one in many instances. Her communication with us was so complete that we rarely had a question or a concern. Cam continued to excel in all his courses, and he gained a great amount of confidence over those two years. His anxiety level seemed to come down within the classrooms and there were very few notes home detailing meltdowns.

Justin and I had decided to get Cam some extra help dealing with his anxiety through outside therapy. Through fifth grade, Cam had biweekly sessions in the evenings with a therapist who worked on confidence, self-help, and coping skills.

Between the efforts of all who were involved, and Cam's natural growth, we saw some progress, but this is something that we still work on to this day.

The fifth and sixth grade middle school was separated into teams, and the classrooms were in pods. This helped all the kids transition from being in one or two classrooms a day in grade school to moving to different classrooms. We had set up a private tour over the summer, and to be honest I was a bit worried. I am horrible with directions and was confused moving through the pod. The special education classroom was on a different floor, which really had me worried. Would Cam be able to navigate the school? We were assured that Cam would have a paraprofessional with him at all times to help him get from class to class. Open house was just a month into the school year, and when we arrived, Cam skillfully took us to each of his classrooms and even introduced us to his teachers—something they had been working on in his social skills class. It was impressive, all of a sudden, he was a *big kid*.

When Cam entered seventh grade, which is in a second middle school building, his anxiety seemed to ramp up. The transition was very hard on him, and often throughout the summer leading up to the start of school, he would cry and say he was going to miss his teacher and his old school. He loved that school, and I believe it is because he gained so much confidence. He had been in an environment that was supportive, and it seemed that was not lost on him.

We talked about his anxiety at length in the IEP meeting for seventh grade, and everyone involved had an idea or two on how to guide him through the transition successfully. As it turned out, the most essential player that year was Cam's paraprofessional (para). Cam has had many wonderful paras over the years, but Mr. Hinton has been the most influential.

His first and most important directive was to understand what made Cam tick. He studied his behaviors, pinpointed anxiety triggers, and worked with every teacher to make sure Cam got the most out of class. If there was ever a school year that Cam needed this kind of detailed attention, it was seventh grade. He was no longer in a special education classroom for reading and language arts; he was in adapted classes for those subjects but continued to have social skills class with the special education teacher. One of Mr. Hinton's goals was to help Cam build more confidence and become a more independent student. Because of his commitment to Cam, their relationship blossomed quickly. Cam absolutely loved Mr. Hinton. I know he felt safe with him.

Mr. Hinton was in constant communication with us, and he even offered us his cell phone number and direct email address. He took it upon himself to create a running shared document where he kept additional notes each day to keep Justin and me in the loop. Anytime Mr. Hinton felt that augmentations were needed in a class, he would consult with the special education teacher, and together they would create a plan to present to the classroom teachers. He was, and still is, one of Cam's biggest fans. The gratitude I have for his chapter in Cam's life is unmeasurable.

Cam has always made good grades in school, an equal mix of As and Bs. That year, he maintained a stellar grade point average, which by the end of the year, landed him on the invitation list for the school's annual academic achievement ceremony held in the school auditorium. This is for all students, not just special needs students, so it was a huge deal. When I told Cam, he was so proud, and to my surprise, did not seem to have any anxiety over the idea of being on stage in front of a packed audience.

When the kids filed onto the stage to take their seats, we found Cam in the crowd. I kept my eyes on him to watch for any discomfort or anxiety. His name was called, and he walked across the floor with confidence to accept his award. What an accomplishment. Luckily, I filled both of my pockets with tissues before leaving the house that day. I needed every last one of them.

Last Woman Standing

I have tried my best to keep things in chronological order, but I do need to take a few steps back to honor one of my personal heroes, Radhika. When I called her five months into Cam's fourth-grade year, she did not hesitate to get back on board. She helped us through the rest of that year and continued to visit the house that summer before Cam was again released from wraparound services. As always, she was incredibly supportive.

She reminded me many times over that I had all the tools I needed, and that the fourth-grade year was not about my skills as a parent, not in the least. I knew she was right. I learned from the best of the best. But still, in the back of my mind, I was terrified to continue the climb without the safety net. There is no doubt in my mind Cam wouldn't be where he is today had she not joined the team. Her commitment to Cam and our family was unwavering. For six years, she attended every evaluation, fought for services, and never missed an IEP meeting. Her treatment plans were ever evolving and pushed Cam to greater heights than we could have imagined. She never once, in all that time, thought Cam was not capable of reaching the goals she set for him.

My time spent watching Radhika work taught me that all the pieces of the puzzle are here. There are days when you will feel like you are building the puzzle under water, some pieces will be harder to find as the tide rolls out and back in again, but you will find them. Just keep looking.

On Radhika's final day, Cam and I decorated the house with colorful streamers, paper flowers, and a giant "thank you" sign that hung across the living room. I ordered a chocolate cake, which I learned over the years was her favorite, and purchased a new brightly colored quilted bag as a gift of appreciation. It didn't feel like enough, but I could have purchased every quilted bag and every chocolate cake on the face of this earth, and it still would not have represented how much she meant to us and how much she was going to be missed.

After the three of us had our cake, Cam headed to the living room to play his video games, and Radhika and I sat at my kitchen table for the next hour pouring over all the work we had done together through laughter and tears. When it was time for her to leave, Cam gave her a huge bear hug. He was almost as tall as her now. She wished him good luck and told him to be a good kid and to remember all the tools he had learned. I could not stop the tears flooding my eyes. He went from a small child in her lap who barely spoke to a young man wishing her good luck in return. I walked her to the door and tried to thank her again, but I could barely speak.

She hugged me and said, "You can do this."

And with that, she was off to work miracles at her next appointment. It was one of the hardest goodbyes I have ever spoken.

The Cam, The Myth, The Legend

As I write this, we are a few weeks into the 2022 school year, and Cam is now 13 years old. He is back to using one-to-three-word sentences. This is not due to our finicky friend autism; he is a teenager. If you ask him how his day was, his answer is "fine." Ask him what he wants to do over the weekend, and you get, "I don't know." How very typical of you Cam!

Like many of his typical peers, he is often on his phone watching YouTubers play the same video games he has collecting dust in the TV cabinet. Why do kids do this? He has a crush on a fellow student but refuses to talk to her and likes to voice his opinion on how stupid he thinks school is. It's quite fun to watch. He does continue to work hard in school, and he has a new para this year who we hope will work out. It is a bit too soon to tell.

He continues to have a social skills class in his curriculum, something Cam still needs. He has always been a bit solitary, but recently he did invite, on his own, a friend to come to the house to play video games. His special education teacher sent me an email because she was so excited for him. She gave my number to the other boy's mom, and that afternoon, we made a plan for the weekend. When his friend (also on the spectrum) arrived, they got straight to it: lots of video game playing, snacks, soda, burping, and complaining about school. It was great. And as a bonus, I got to spend time chatting with the boy's mom. It's always good to be with people who get it.

Cam still loves to build things. There are always scraps of cardboard, paper, springs from pens, and other various debris lying around his room. He also loves to fold origami. I'm not talking your average crane, but very complex origami. He can follow a tutorial online once, fold a piece of paper an unimaginable number of times, and then recreate the piece without watching the video ever again. Our house is covered in mini paper creations, including jeeps, boats, backpacks, frogs, umbrellas, flowers, transforming ninja stars, anime characters—yes anime characters—and so much more. I honestly think it's Cam's answer to those damn tea towels that would never comply.

He also loves to create comic strips. He has a bin of notebooks under his bed filled with comics he has drawn and written. This has been going on for several years. Most often, the stories involve him and Gabby traveling the world on adventures. Sometimes, a favorite cartoon character or two will enter the mix. He is a great storyteller, and his imagination continues to impress us and his teachers alike.

He zips around the house on his hoverboard—something I had put off getting him even though he had wanted one for years. I don't know why I was so worried; the kid still has amazing balance. As soon as the thing was charged, he stepped onto it and took off, not so much as a wobble.

Over the past few years, we have come to realize that Cam has a fantastic singing voice; his range is incredible. He still loves to remix popular songs on a whim or belt them out operatic style ... and it works. We placed him in chorus class this year, the thought was that (1) he has a great voice, so why not and (2) the class would be a great sensory input session during his day since vocal stims are still very much a part of his life.

He is now a few weeks into to eighth grade, and his daily notes show that he is actually having trouble in chorus.

When I asked him about it, he said, "The teacher keeps telling me to blend in. She wants me to be like everybody else, but I am an individual."

"OK, yes Cam, but the point of a chorus is to work as a team!"

I reached out to the teacher who said that for the most part Cam follows directions but at times he sings in a "silly voice, almost like a batman voice." I hate to say it, but I could not think of anything better than a batman voice chorus, so I was not sure how to respond appropriately. I did have a talk with Cam, so we shall see how things go.

His overall transition into eighth grade has been a little rough. He tells us he misses Mr. Hinton, his para from seventh grade, and even though Justin and I are a bit worried, history tells us that things will shake out for Cam. Another fun fact is that Cam can do complex math in his head, which is pretty cool. However, there has been a constant battle between him and his math teachers over the past few years because math teachers, rightfully so, want to see how students find the solutions to the equations. We don't make a big deal of it; we don't throw out math questions just to watch him solve them quickly in his head. It's simply something he can do.

Gabby and Cam continue to be thick as thieves but also get into fights and insult battles the way typical siblings do.

Gabby used to tell Cam that once he was taller than her, she was going to beat him up, to which he always replied, "I'd like to see you try."

Cam is currently an inch shorter than her, so he better watch out. Gabby has always been a tiny little thing with big sky-blue eyes and rosy cheeks, as if she was born with the perfect shade of blush. Don't let these sweet features fool you; she is as sharp as a tack, a fierce advocate, and a true spitfire. She often reminds me of my mom.

She recently left for college and is interested in studying law and civil rights. She will blaze trails, no doubt.

Leading up to her departure, Cam would get quite upset and say things like "I don't want Gabby to leave," and "I will miss Gabby."

138

During her senior year, she said that she would stay home and commute to a local school. Gabby was worried about who would take care of Cam after school since she had been his babysitter both after school and over the summer months for several years now. Although I was impressed and proud of the young woman she was becoming, I could not let her add the college experience to her list of sacrifices made for her little brother.

At the time, my commute to work was over an hour. I realized one way to make Gabby feel more comfortable with moving away to school would be to quit my job and find something much closer to home, so that's what I did. By some cosmic event I found a job so close to home that my commute is under a minute, and I also have the option to work from home ... perfect. On the days Justin worked in the office, he made it a point to be home in time to get Cam off the bus. He did this for the rest of that school year, relieving Gabby of her duties. Together we successfully convinced our daughter that she could safely leave her little brother alone with Mom and Dad.

When it came time for college applications, Gabby applied to five schools and was accepted into all of them with each offering academic scholarships. We were beyond proud, and the icing on the cake was that her college essay was a brilliant and poignant look at what life is like with a special needs sibling and the lessons she has learned. Thankfully, Cam has adjusted well to her move. He started school soon after she started, so there was much to distract him. The university she chose is only about 30 minutes away from us, and we see her when she comes home to work a weekend job. Every once in a while, Cam will FaceTime her for a few minutes just to get his Gabby fix. I admit, I do it too.

Cam is still very funny. He loves a good prank or a quick-witted joke. His sarcasm is often brilliant and keeps us on our toes. Some of his comebacks, although not meant to be funny, are hilarious. Not long ago, I asked Cam to clean up all the paper scraps in his room that started to make their way into the hallway via his socks. He had left a few "snibbles," as we call them, behind, so I offered him the vacuum cleaner. He said under his breath, "Your cleanliness standards are a bit high." We do have to be careful when laughing at these types of comments because Cam can often misconstrue it as us laughing at him. In reality, it is more of a reaction to the once upon a time nonverbal label.

Over the last few years, Justin, Gabby, and I have focused on life skills with Cam. I will randomly announce "life skills" and walk Cam through things like watering the plants or folding laundry. He has learned to cook simple things, which was born more so out of Gabby getting tired of making lunch for him over the summer. I came home one day to find Cam making himself a grilled cheese sandwich.

"When did this start?" I asked.

To which Gabby replied, "When I got sick of making grilled cheese."

He helps around the house when asked, not so much independently, but again, he's a teenager. He still likes to keep to himself, and after school, he typically heads to his room. I think it is a time of decompression for him, and we let him have that. There are times he will invite Justin or me to do something with him, and it can be anything from trying out a new origami creation to playing video games. Well, he used to ask me to play video games, but I am terrible at them. At first, he would tell me, "It's OK, Mum; you are learning." But over time, he asked me less and less. I can't blame him; I am really awful at them. It seems recently he prefers Justin over me in general. It used to be Gabby over us all, but I am fine with it.

I think Justin, out of all of us, has sacrificed the most. For a good portion of Cam's rapid progress, Justin was working two jobs to keep us afloat. He missed a lot of firsts with Cam, and even though I tried my best to keep him in the fold with videos, in-the-moment text messages, and phone calls, it's not the same as being there. But Justin never complained. He never put himself first; that is just his nature. Without Justin's unwavering drive to provide for our family and make sure everyone else got what they needed, we would not be where we are today. I am sure of it. His work schedule is far different than it was back then, and he often works from home. He has taken over most of Cam's care. Everything from packing his lunch and morning routines to homework and random checks to make sure Cam is on point with his personal hygiene. I find myself feeling a bit guilty some days because I seem to just be laying back at times.

For many years, I thought that I was the parent who knew how to best care for Cam. I think this is common with special needs parents: there is usually one parent who attends most of the therapies and appointments while the other one makes sure there is a roof over everyone's head. Naturally, the therapy parent feels the most responsible for following through, simply because of all the time put in. But at some point, we have to let go of ego and understand how important it is to ask for help.

Sharing in the caretaking not only gives us some time to rest, but also shows our spouse or family members that we trust and need them. Honestly, it took me too long to come to this realization, and it seems now, that I've let go a bit, my relationship with Justin is stronger. I think this time was meant for Cam and Justin, and it is nice to sit back and watch the boys do their thing. The two of them have a wonderful bond. They are both silly as hell, love to watch anime, and are huge *Star Wars* fans. Justin and Cam get into incredibly detailed storytelling and sometimes have contests to see who can write the best comic strip.

I know that Justin had concerns about what their relationship would look like when Cam was diagnosed, and he will tell you, he had big plans when we found out we were having a son. Justin did not have a father figure growing up. He was excited to create the bond he saw between his friends and their dads as a kid. Fishing and camping trips, sporting events, and football and soccer practices on chilly Saturday mornings were on the agenda. I recently asked Justin what he would say to another dad who just got the diagnosis. He said, "It's OK. Your relationship may not look like what you planned, and although you may find that some of those things work— better yet—you will find things that are truly unique to you and your son."

In other news, Cam has been letting a few swear words slip. I'm shocked it took him this long, considering my vocabulary.

A while back, when I accidentally put two straws in Cam's cup (he will only drink from straws or a water bottle), he said, "Holy shit, two straws!"

Once while playing a video game, he got really pissed and threw the controller to the ground.

"Whoa kiddo, what happened?" I asked.

He responded, "I got fucking bamboozled."

Oh boy, I had to turn away and compose myself. I mean here we are, the once nonverbal kid using the words *fucking* and *bamboozled* appropriately. How mad could I really get? Once I thought I could get a word out without laughing, we had a nice long talk about swear words. He has not let much slip since then. Although, this past summer we went to our favorite lake for a weekend trip. Cam, Gab, and I were floating around in our inner tubes. I got out and ran up to the room to get some drinks, and when I came back, Gabby and Cam were laughing hysterically.

Of course, I prodded "What's going on!"

Gabby told Cam, "Do it to mom. Do it to mom."

Cam said, "No way."

He was not going to show me whatever it was that had Gabby in stitches.

I pleaded with him and finally he said, "Fine. Look, a duck!"

I looked around but didn't see this duck. When I looked back at Cam, he had both of his middle fingers resting on the outside of his tube with a giant grin on his face. There was no gaining my composure. My son just flipped me the double bird, and I laughed so hard I choked. You win some; you lose some. He is a teenager after all.

Cam still has very strong opinions on how things should be or work. He can get pretty upset when things don't go according to plan. There are still times in school when he just wants to do his own thing and struggles to follow directions. He is a bit of a picky eater and dislikes anything messy. He was never one for finger painting or playing in the mud. He is very regimented with time. He asks what's for lunch at exactly 11 a.m. every day and what's for dinner at exactly at 4 p.m. He still worries about timing and how long things will take.

Justin and I made the decision to start him on a low dose of antianxiety medication late last year. We have seen marked improvement in how he responds to situations that in the past would send him into a tizzy. It was another hard decision for us to make, but after years of trying different therapies, we decided that now was the time, especially with hormones raging. So far, we are happy with the results and are keeping a very close eye on things. He has held on to several of his original self-stimulatory behaviors, though. The vocal and verbal stimming, as well as darting from one corner of a room to another, are his favorites. Around eight years old, I started talking to Cam about his stims. It seemed he was at a point where I could explain to him what they are and why he does them. I wanted him to feel comfortable in the event someone outside of our circle has something to say about it.

He seemed to understand, and when he would be very involved in a stim, I would say, "Cam, what are up to?"

He would say, "Just stimming around."

I have asked him what the stims do for him and his reply has always been, "They make me happy."

Who can argue with that? He can often stop if you ask him to, and there are times that we do, especially at night when we are trying to get to sleep, and he is singing a Taylor Swift lyric operatic style over and over from his bedroom. We blame Gabby for this one; she is a huge Taylor Swift fan. I think the timing of the conversation was just right. Any time we talk to Cam about his autism now, he seems to feel as though it is only a part of who he is and is unapologetic for his differences, which has always been a goal of mine for him.

Even though Cam tends to hang out with Dad most days, there are times he chooses me to watch the latest gaming video with him, or he will pull out an old board game we used to play. I try very hard to be present in these moments. So much of my relationship with Cam has been centered around therapies and reaching goals, and now it seems we get to just be. That is not to say that we did not have fun times while he was growing up. We did. But now we just get to be ourselves in those moments.

Sometimes Cam will even choose to sit next to me on the couch and put his head on my shoulder. It's rare so when he does this, I don't move a muscle for fear he will move away—almost like we do when our kids are babies and sleeping in our arms. We don't want to risk waking them up by moving or even breathing. In a sense, his current lack of interest in me has caused me to cherish these special moments.

Cam and I still have a very strong connection. We have been through so much together, there is a part of this life that only he and I have navigated, and those around us have only experienced second hand. We spent countless hours side by side in therapies and evaluations, visits with Dr. T., our daily routine of sensory diets, and endless follow through after all the appointments were finished for the day. He knows that I am always available to him, that I will never stop advocating for him or give up thinking outside of the box to help him through any obstacle. It is unspoken, and in this case, I am OK with the silence.

146

We were paired together by some universal force, and there are no words that can truly describe our connection. My relationship with Cam has created, in me, the ability to be accepting of what is. Every season, when the leaves begin to fall and the air turns cold, I think of the ride home the day Cam was diagnosed. The bare branches of winter hold an echo of the fear that followed me home that day. I have come to understand that the leaves must fall to allow new growth in the next season. We must let go every once in a while, just as the trees do. If we miss this step, try to hold on to every fear or every expectation of what should be, we are not giving the next season the space to bloom.

My biggest hope for Cam is that he never feels the need to apologize for his differences, and that he is comfortable with who he is.

When I told him that I was writing a book about him, he looked at me and said "Why?"

I said, "Good grief Cam! Because you have worked so hard and have beaten so many odds."

He said, "That's just me. I'm Cam."

Mission accomplished, for now. By no means do I think we are at a resting point. Teenage years followed by young adulthood will present a whole new set of challenges to face and mountains to conquer. We have the gear, and we will continue the climb as a family. As for Cam, he will make it to the top because, well ... he is Cam.

About the Author

What business does a mother of two with a background in real estate and commercial lending have writing a book about autism? This is a question Carrie P. Holzer has asked herself many times over. But after eleven years of being told, at every turn, to share her son Cam's story, she has made it her business.

When the COO of the company Carrie works for was told she had written a book about her son and hadn't published it yet, he gifted Carrie the funds on behalf of the company to have the book published. The gift further assured Carrie that her family's journey is an impactful one and should be shared.

As a first-time author, Carrie uses an honest lens to create a feeling of support and connection for her readers, bringing to life her humorous take on the highs and lows of life with autism.

Carrie, her husband Justin, and their two children, Cam and Gabby, live in the suburbs of Pittsburgh, Pa. Although the family's commitment to help Cam along the winding road of autism is ever present, recent years have allowed them to slow down a bit. With therapies falling away as Cam reaches goal after goal, the family has more time for weekend trips to their favorite lake spot, hitting golf balls at the local driving range, and Sunday afternoon video game matches.

Connect with Carrie at www.carriepholzer.com or on Facebook or Instagram.

CPSIA information can be obtained
at www.ICGtesting.com
Printed in the USA
LVHW021325160423
744468LV00005B/677